# Large Coloring Patterns

By: Kate Stevens

This publication is part of a series of products and publications.

**Copyright 2017 Kate Stevens.**

ALL RIGHTS RESERVED. One or more global copyright treaties protect the information in this document. This Special Report is not intended to provide exact details or advice. This report is for informational purposes only. Author reserves the right to make any changes necessary to maintain the integrity of the information held within. This Special Report is not presented as legal or accounting advice. All rights reserved, including the right of reproduction in whole or in part in any form. No parts of this book may be reproduced in any form without written permission of the copyright owner.

NOTICE OF LIABILITY

In no event shall the author or the publisher be responsible or liable for any loss of profits or other commercial or personal damages, including but not limited to special incidental, consequential, or any other damages, in connection with or arising out of furnishing, performance or use of this book.

# Introduction

Coloring relieves stress

Coloring may sound like a simple activity, but more and more people are discovering that it is an effective stress reliever and mood booster. Some psychologists have even said that coloring is a form of meditation.

Creative activities benefit seniors

Research studies show that engaging seniors in creative activities like coloring can improve their health, lead to fewer doctor visits, reduce medication, and decrease the number of health problems.

You can benefit from coloring too! It is a quick and inexpensive way to help you relax and engage in a fun and creative activity for as much or as little time as you have.

Creative activities benefit everyone

Improves moods
Relieves stress
Reduces agitation
Promotes socialization
Provides an outlet for self-expression
Helps to maintain motor function
Improves dexterity (grip control)
Improves hand-eye coordination
Encourages cooperation
Promotes mindfulness (full attention & concentration required)
Provides a sense of accomplishment

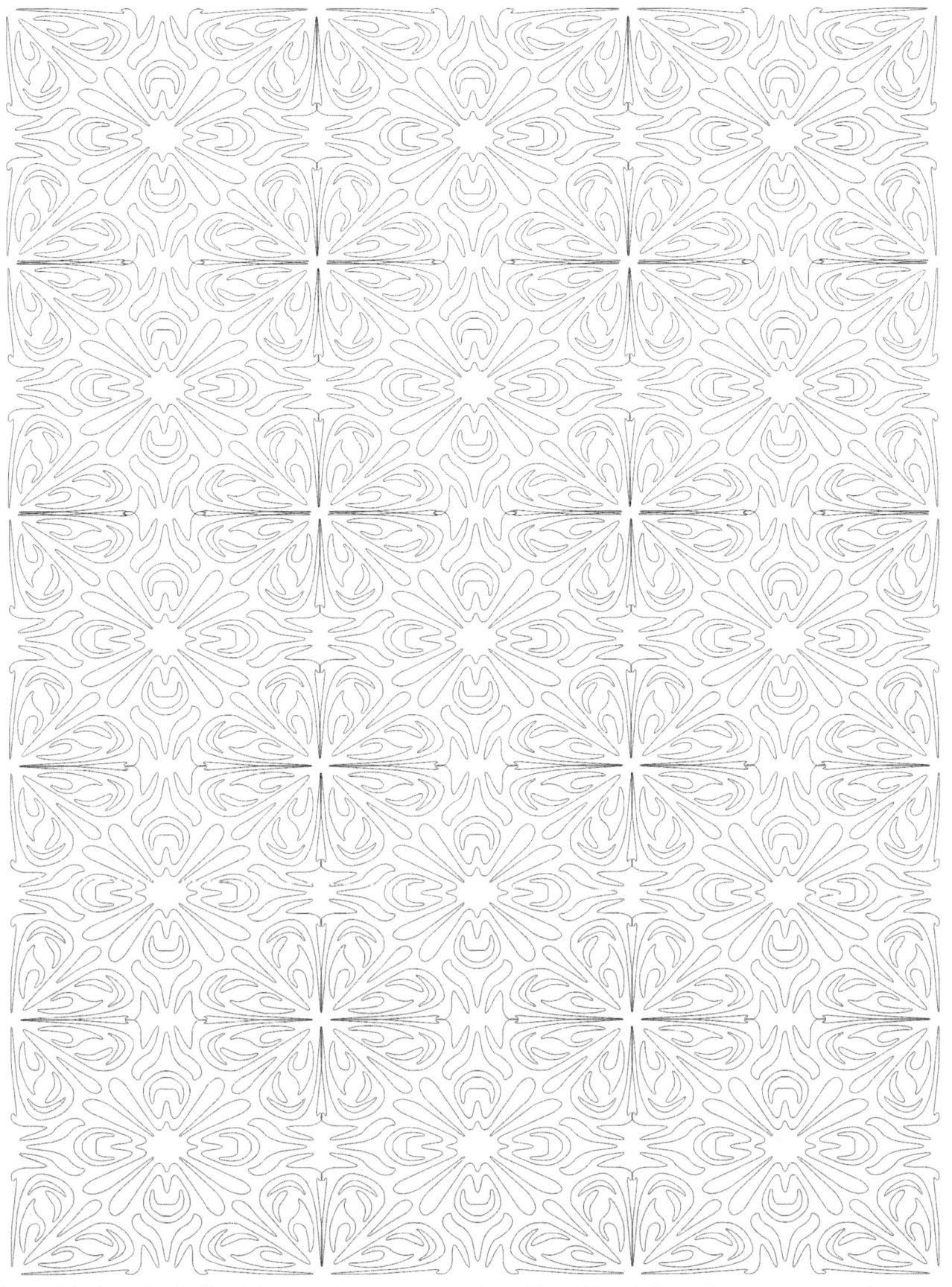

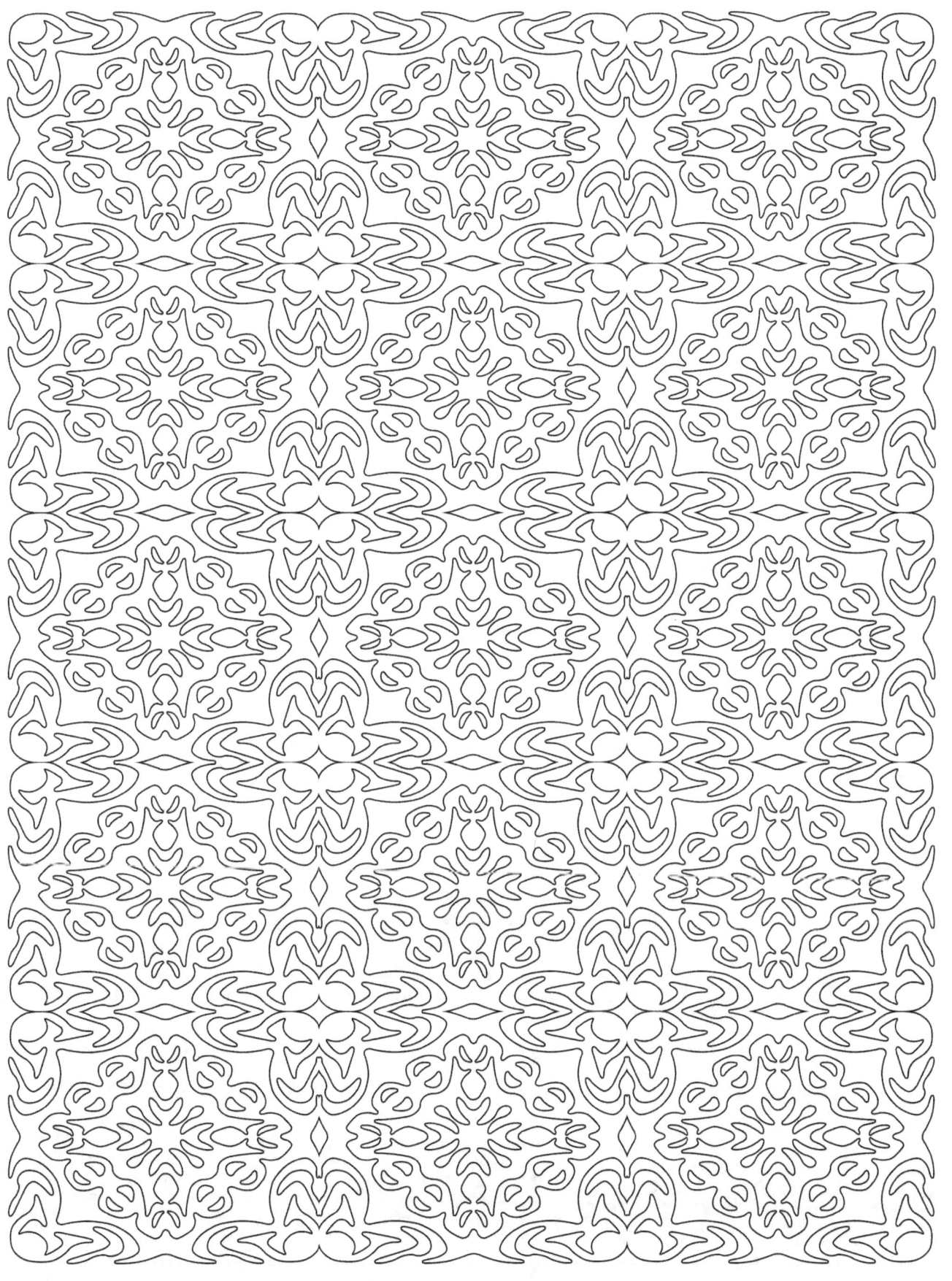

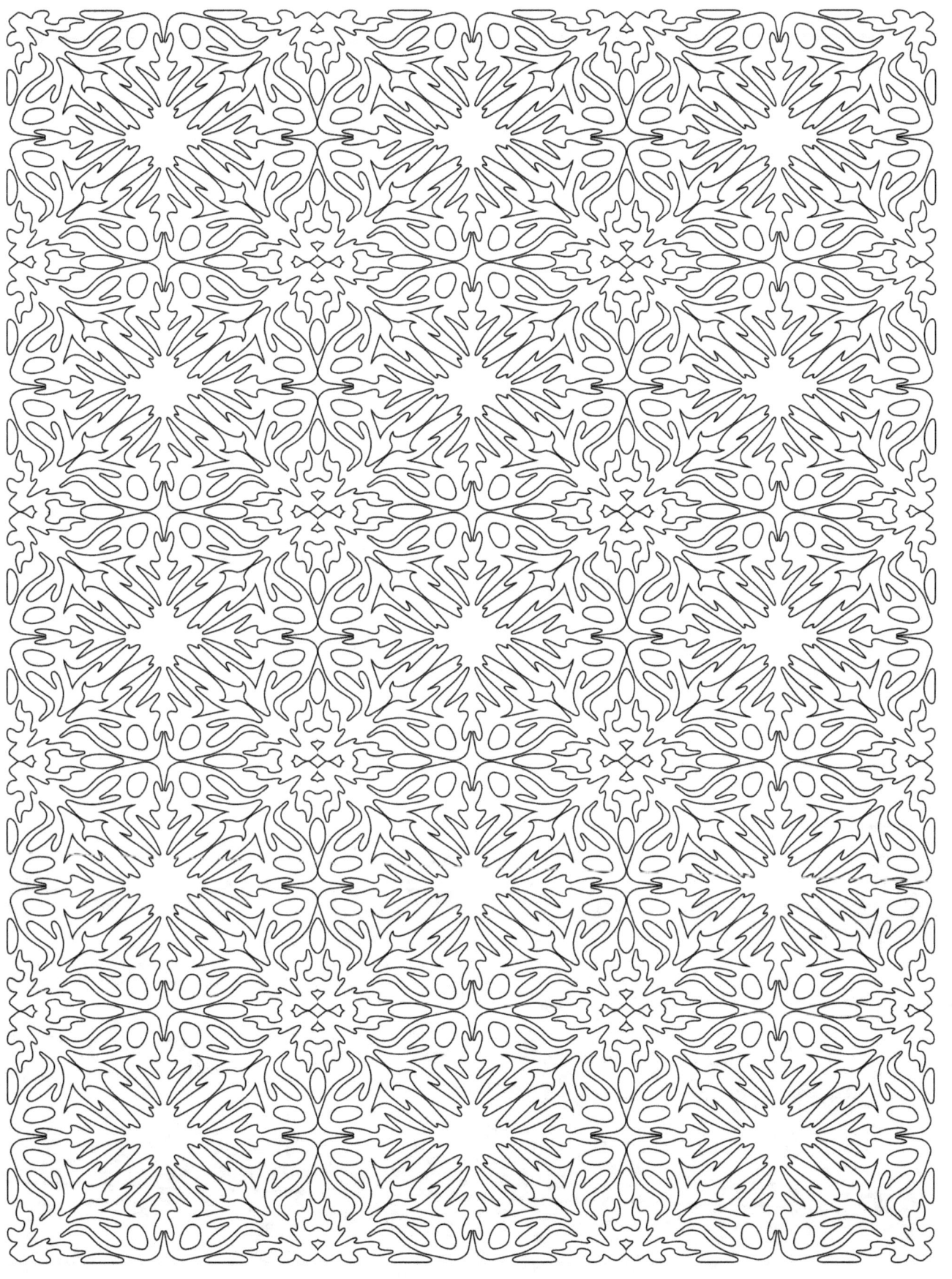

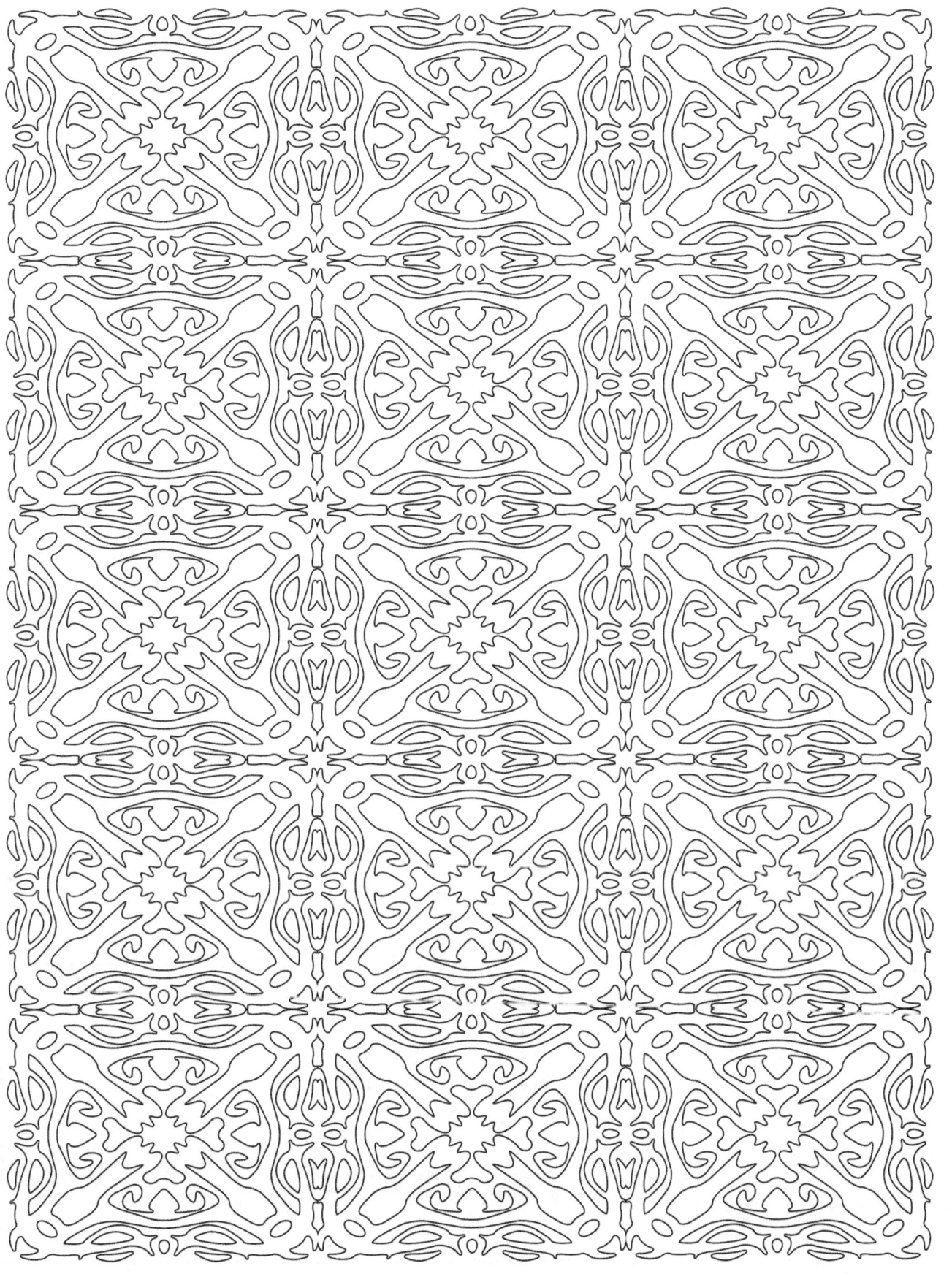

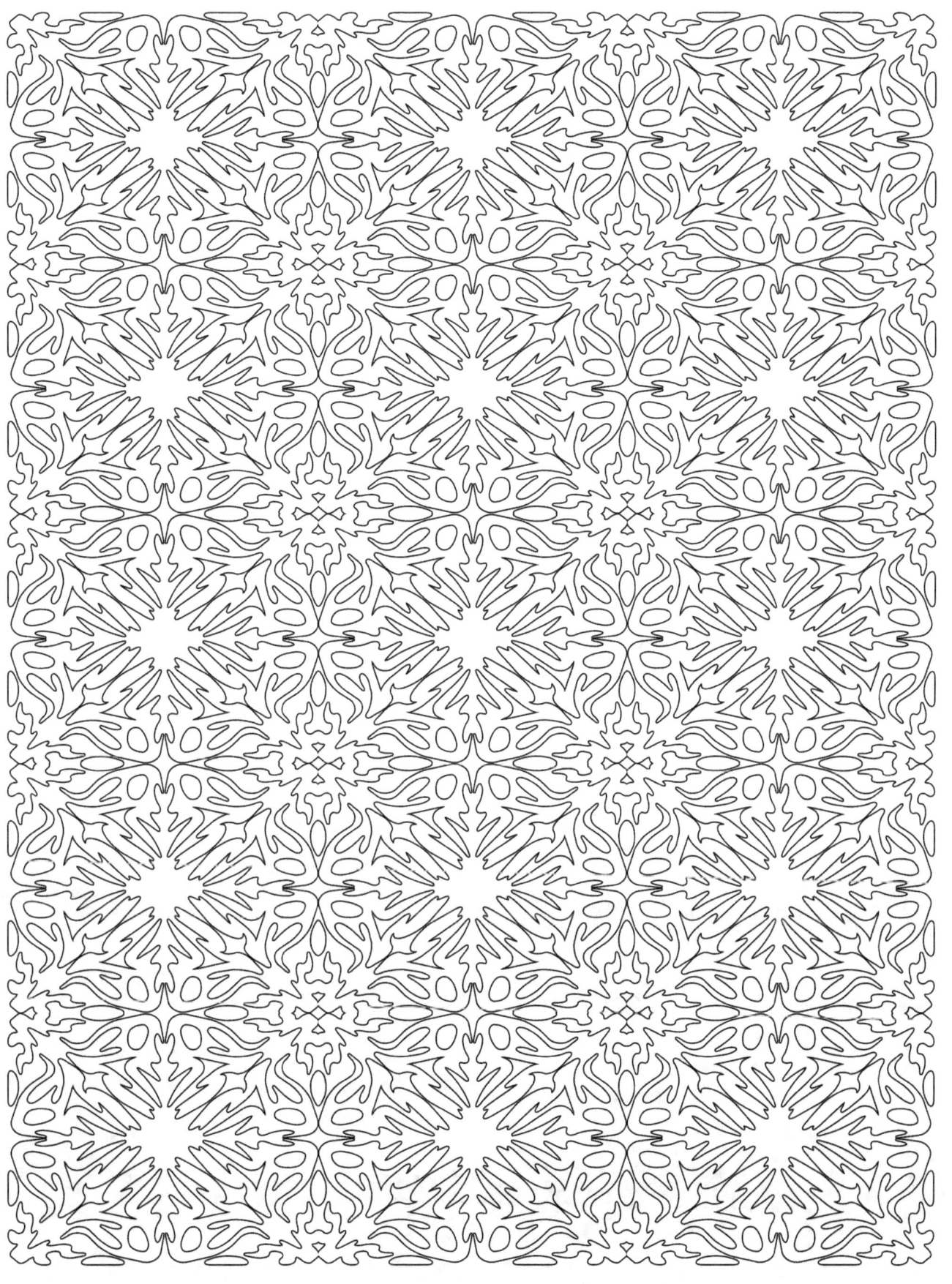

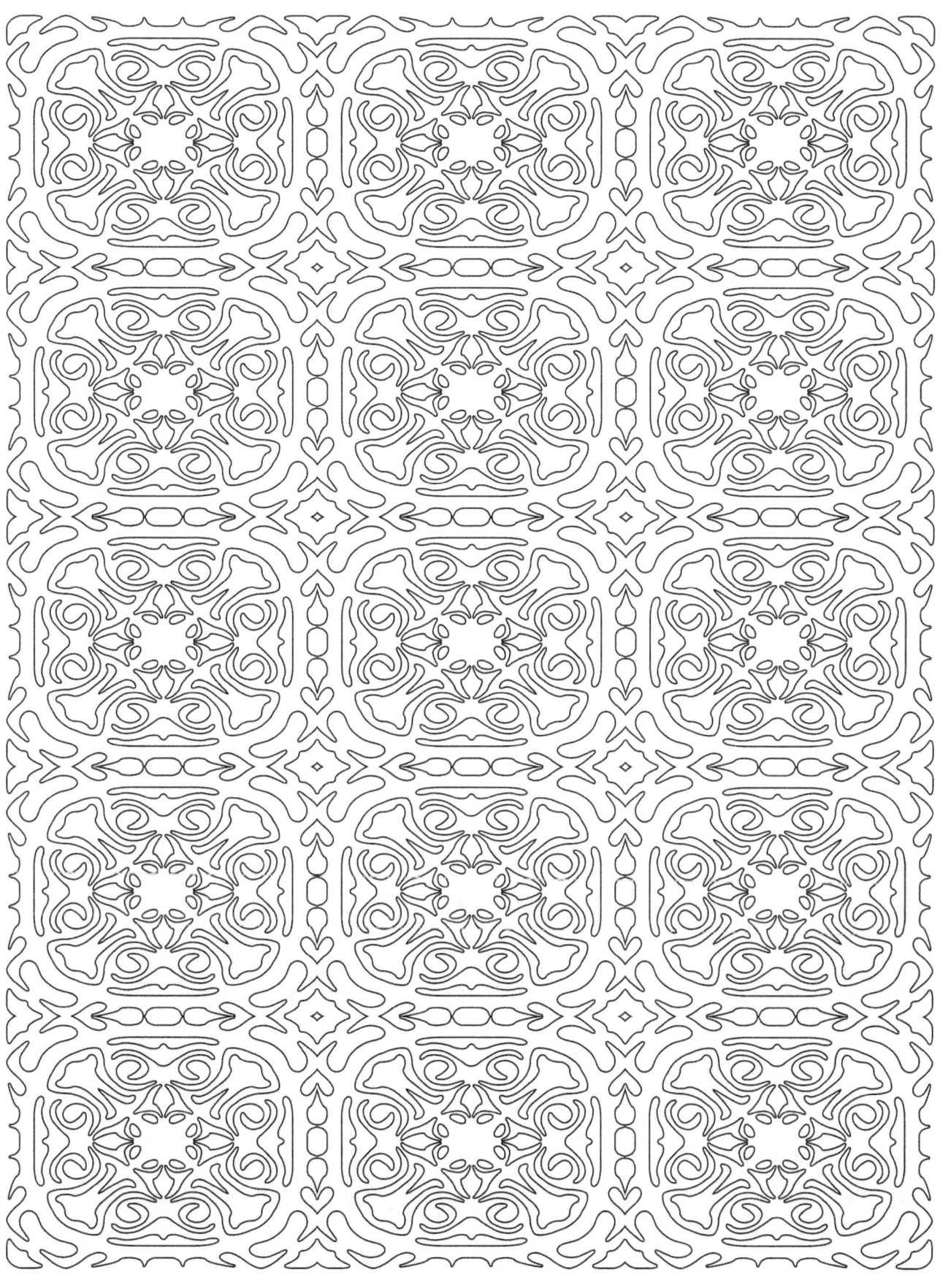

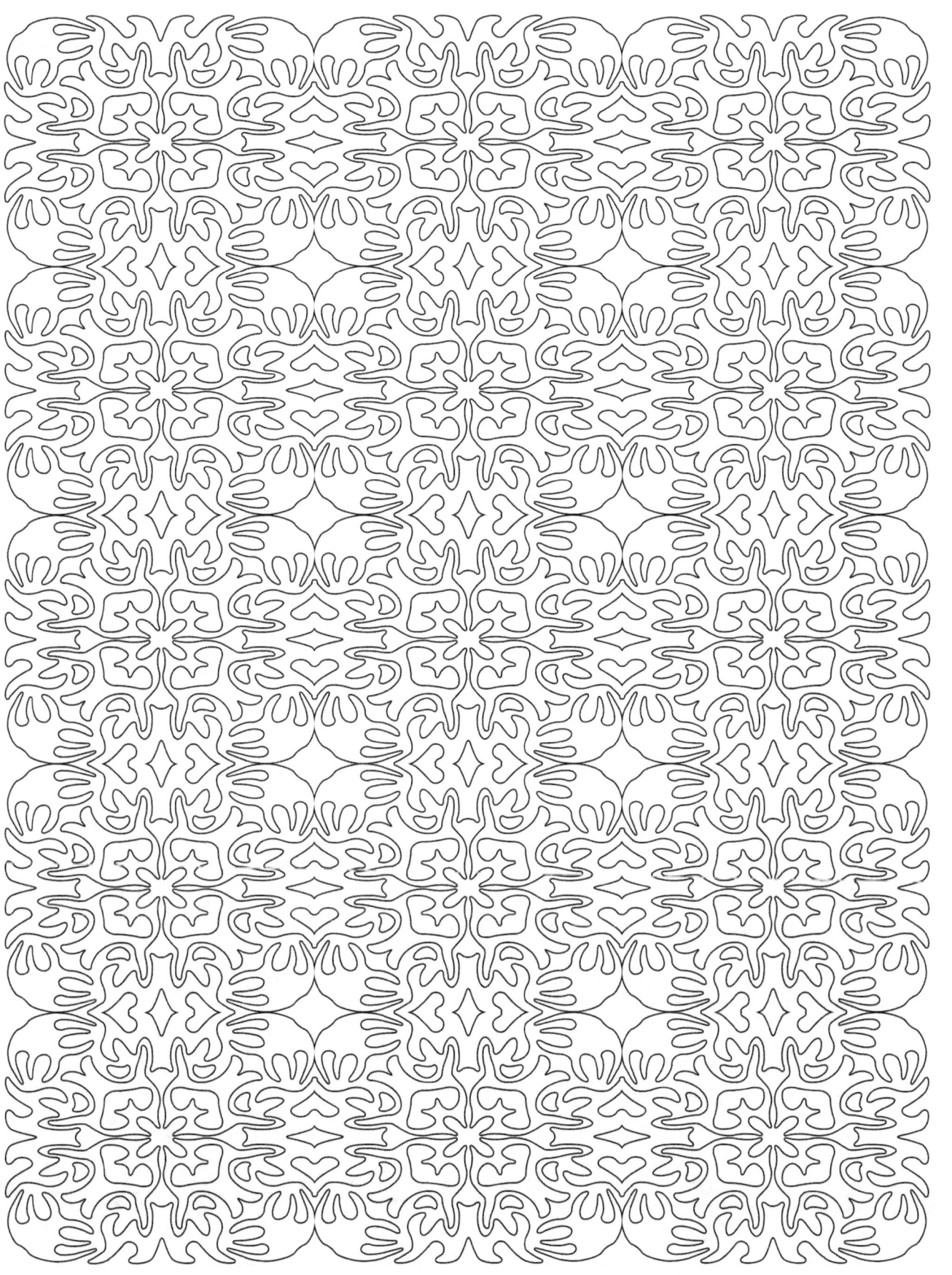

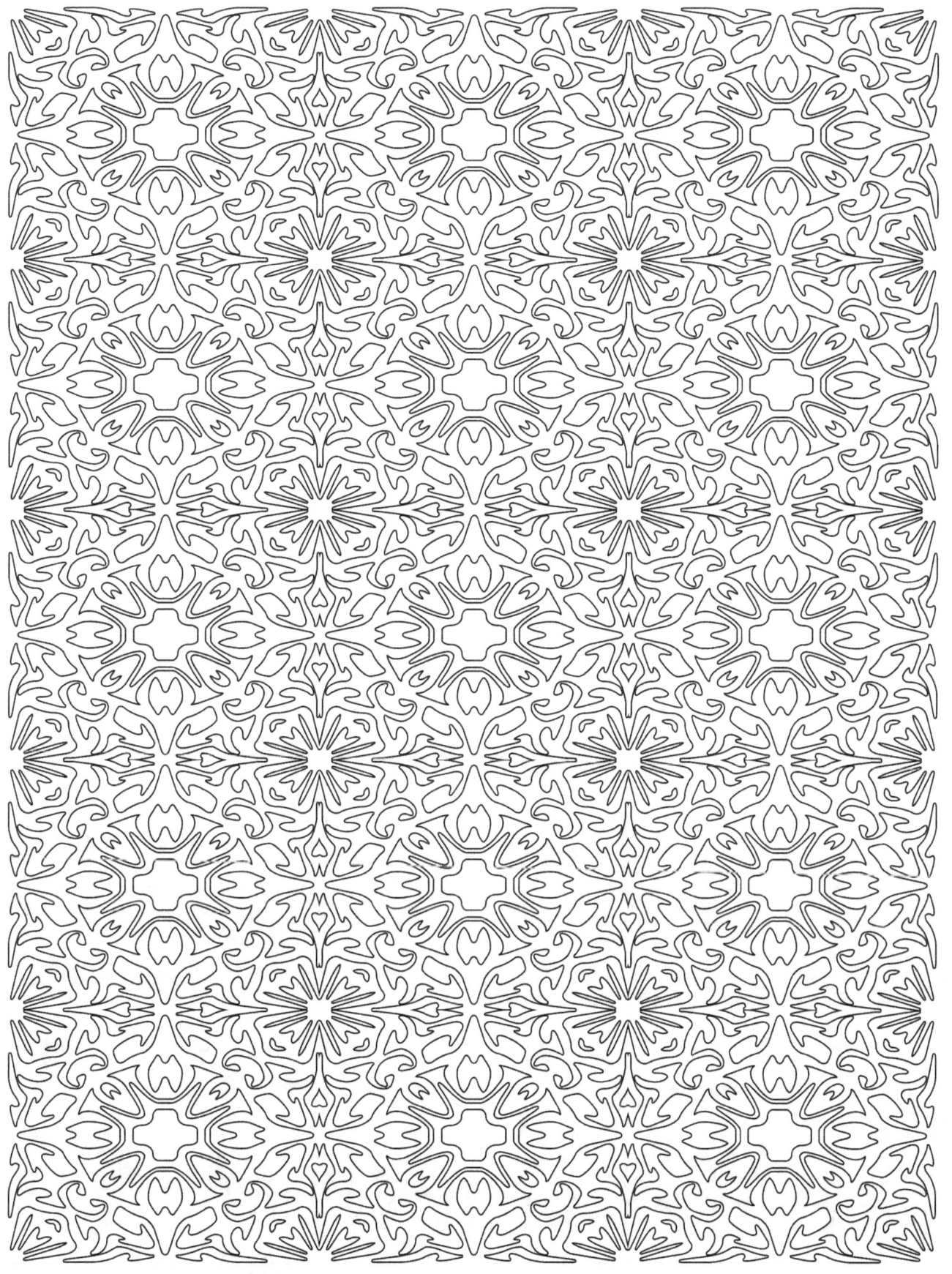

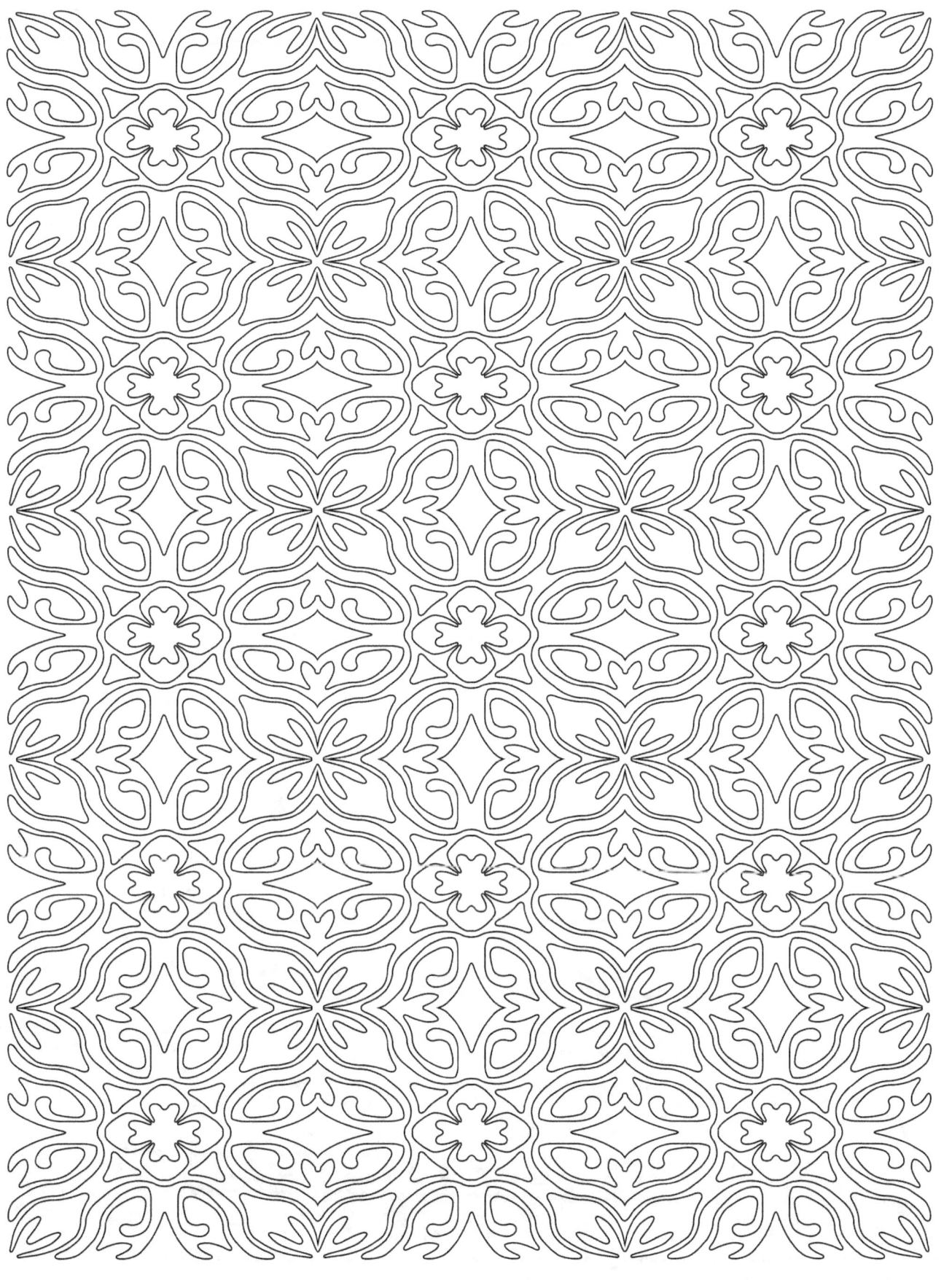

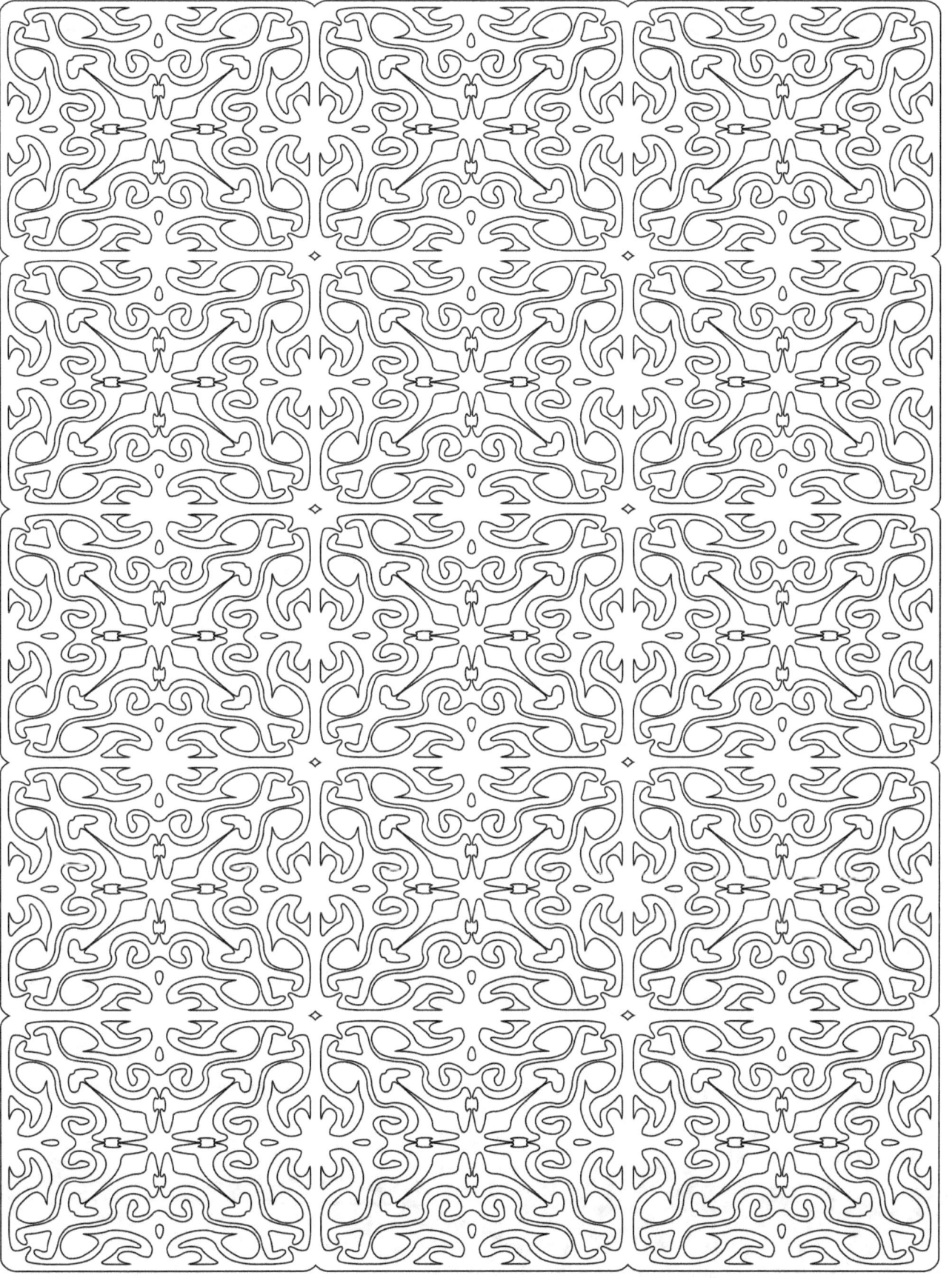

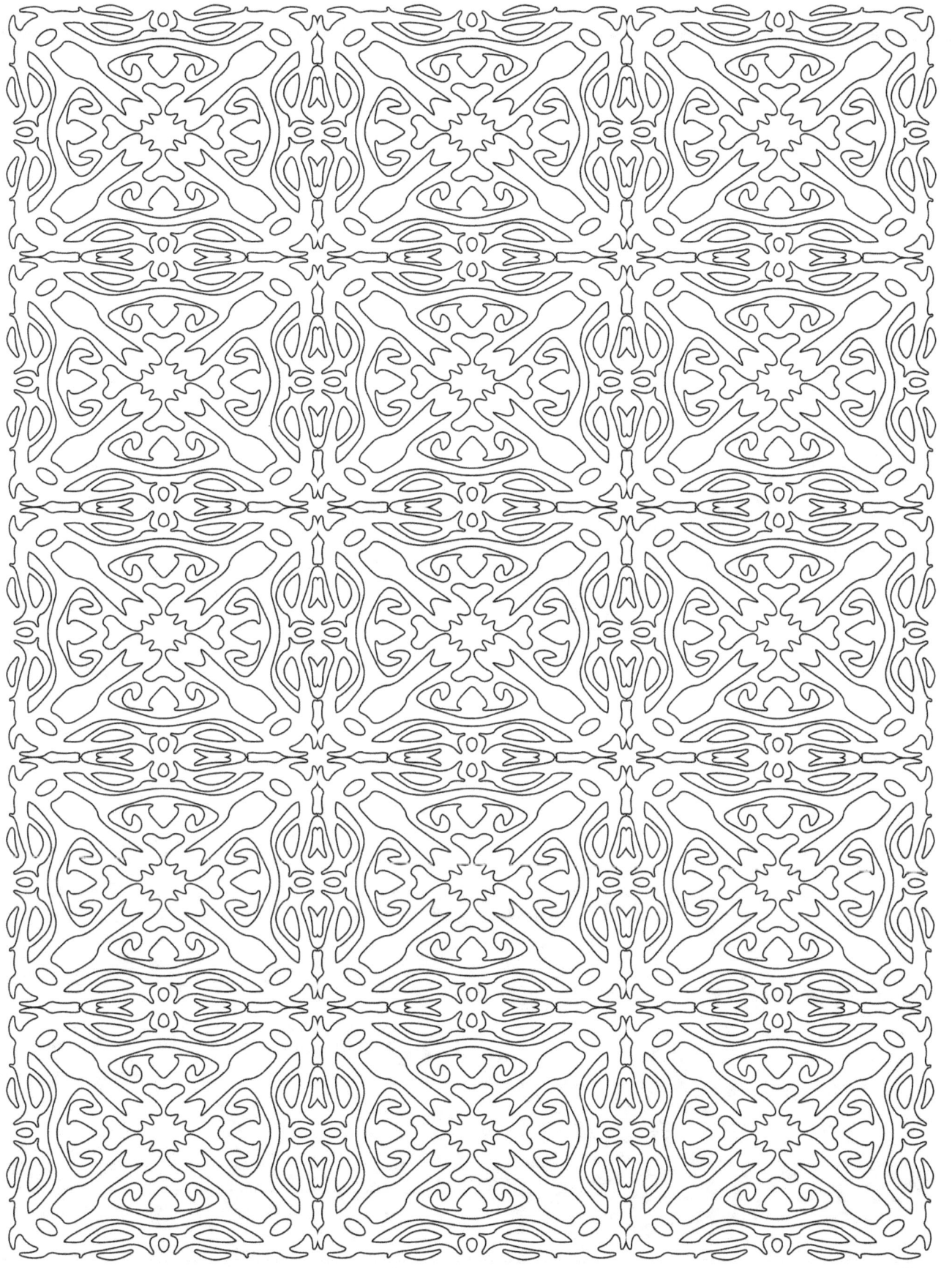

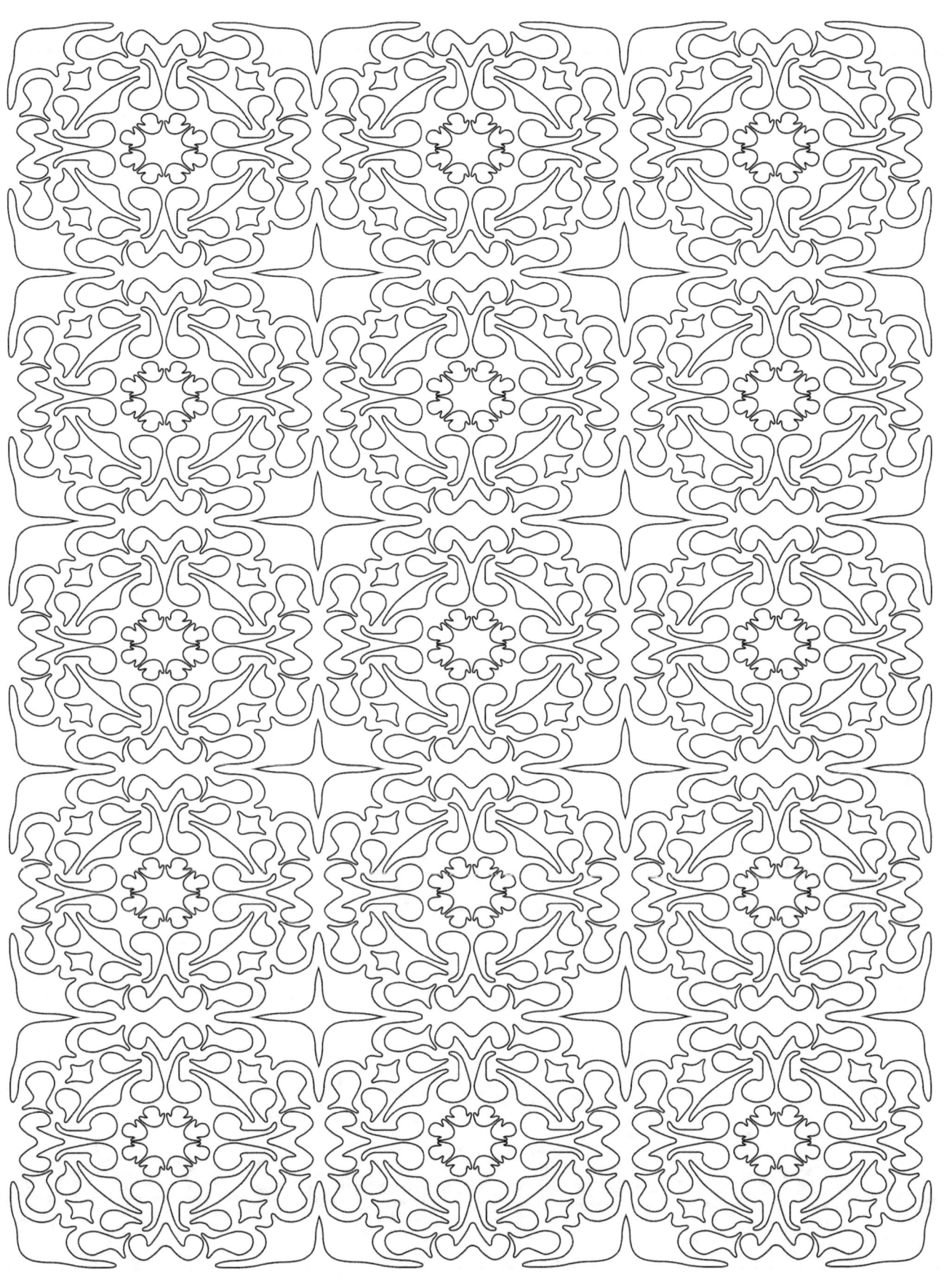

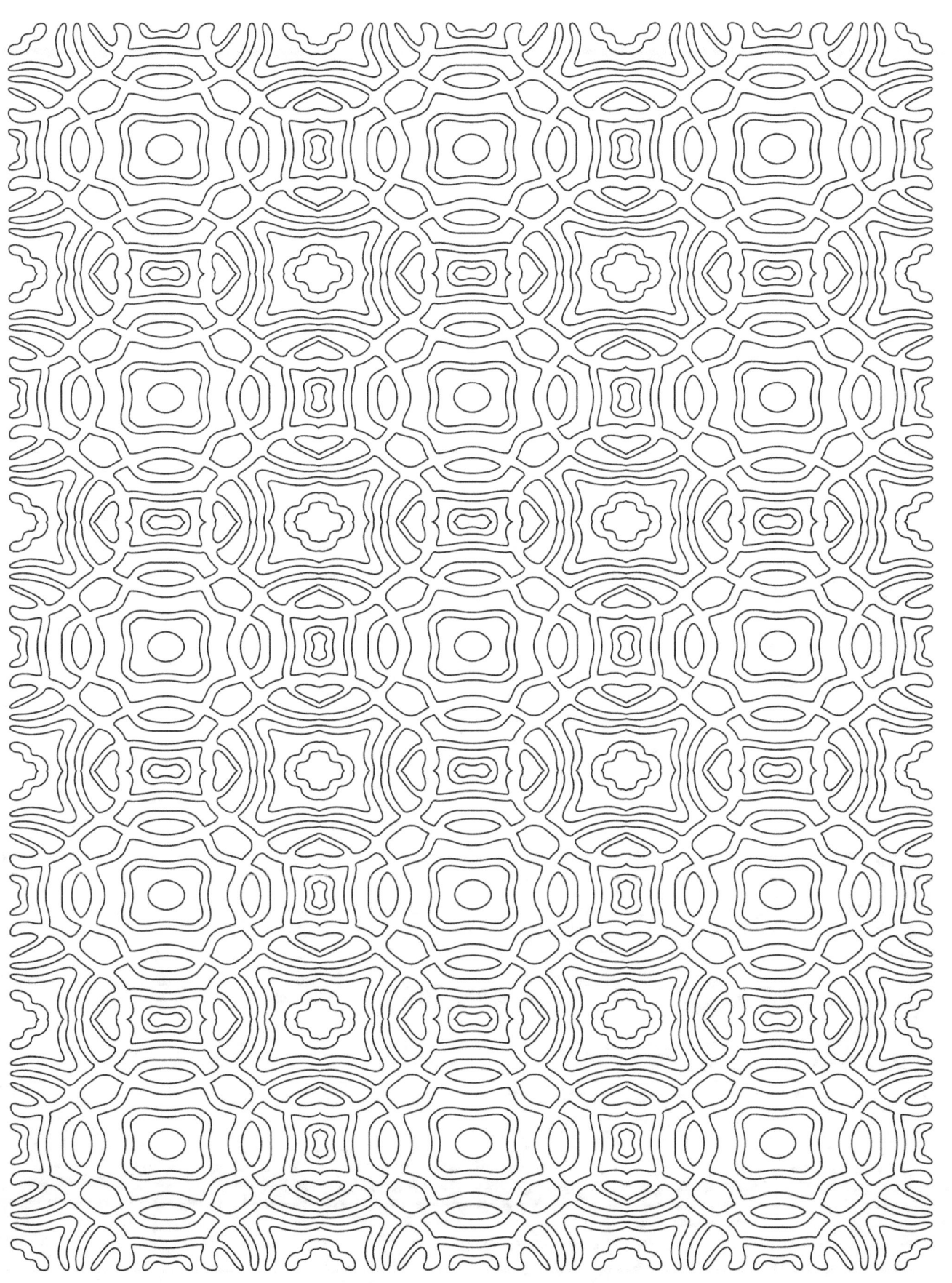

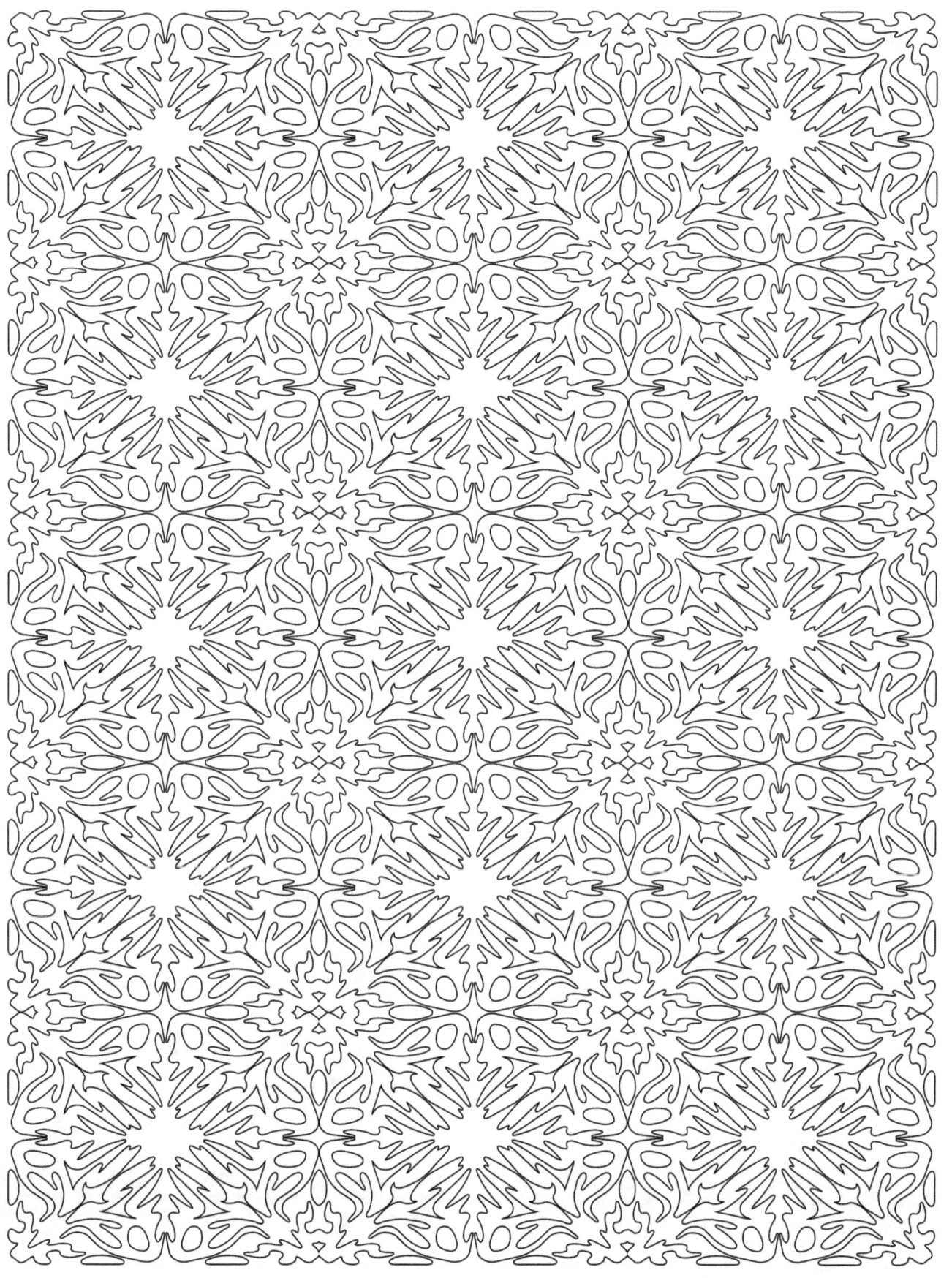

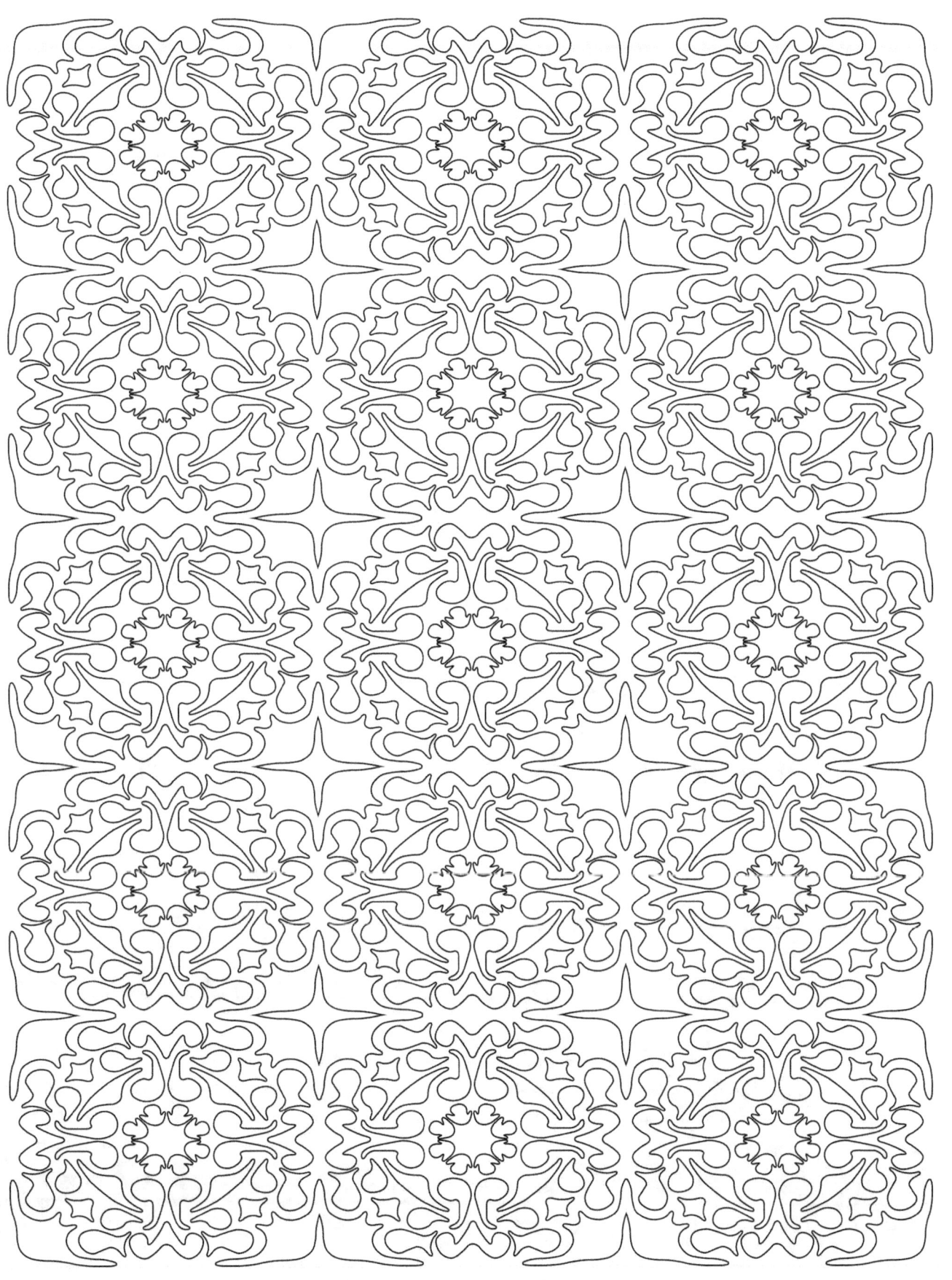

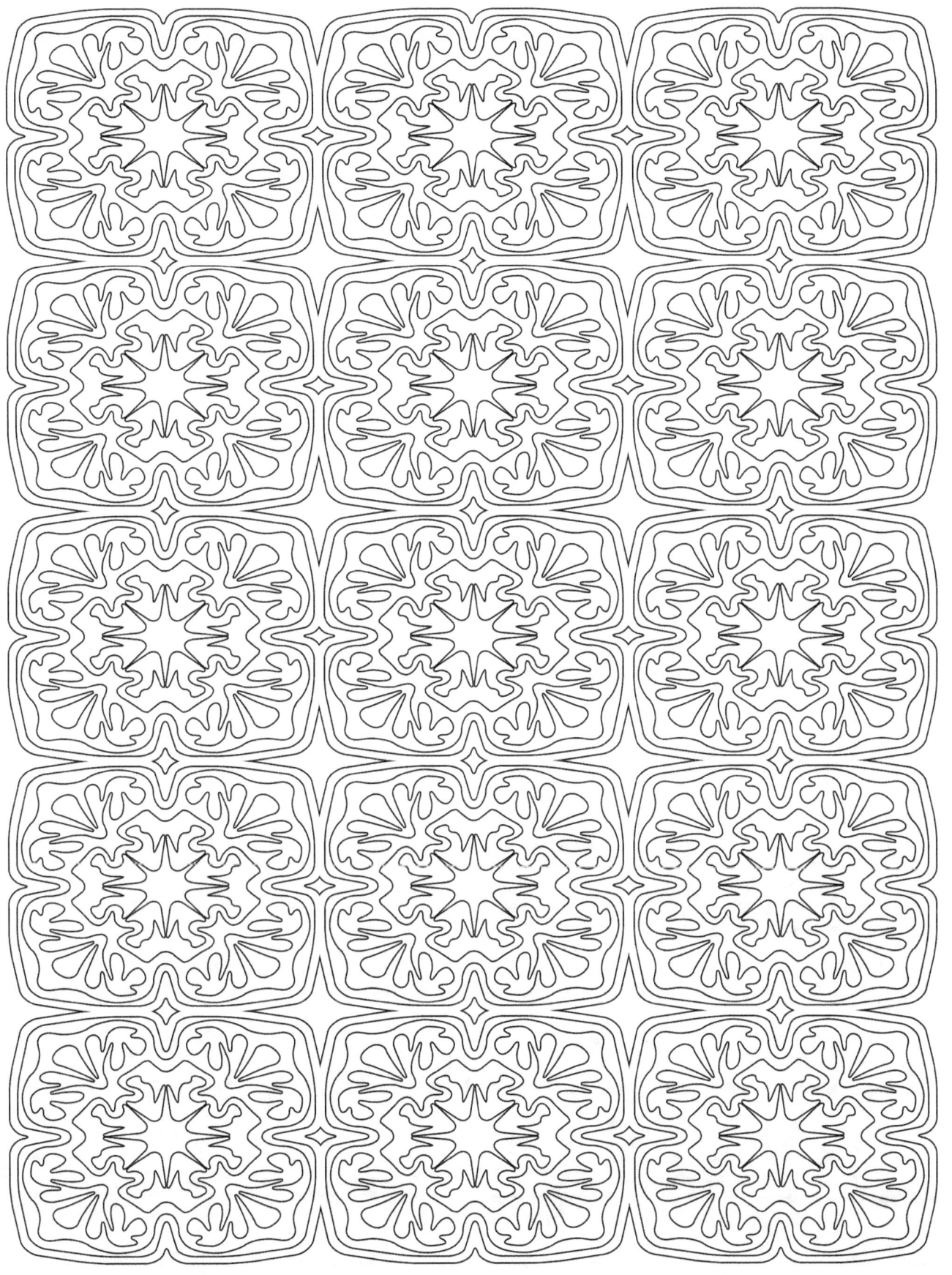

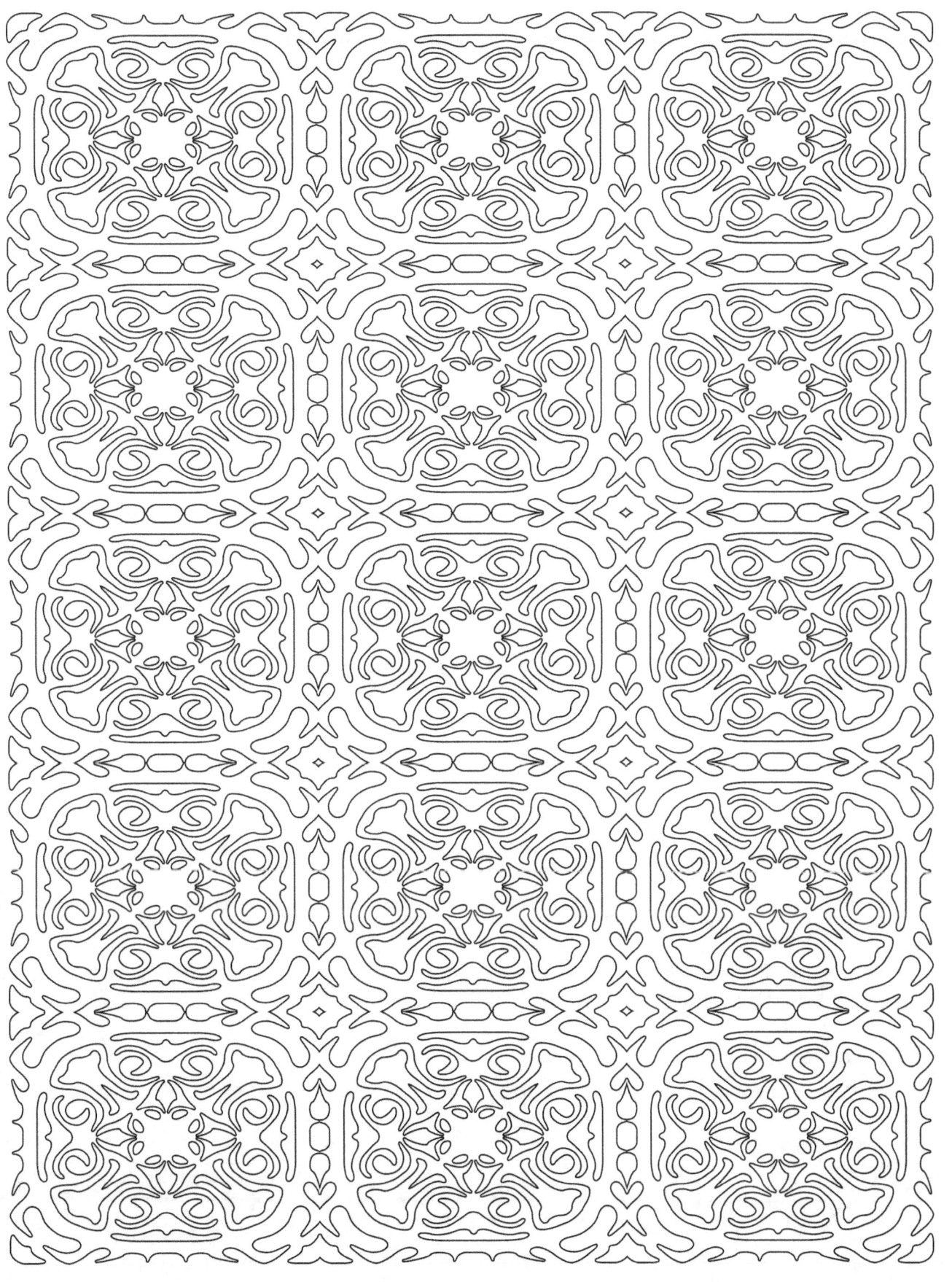

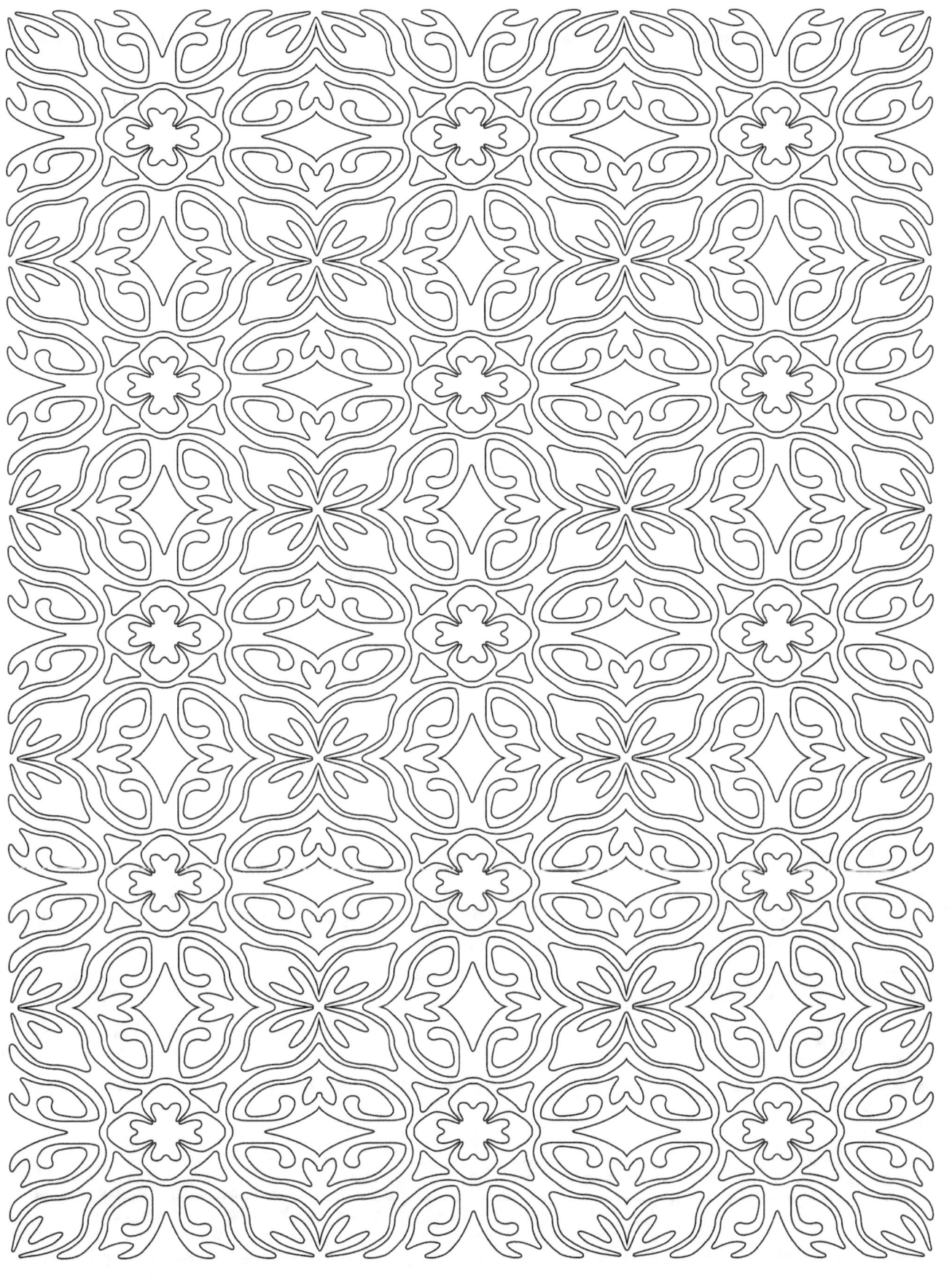

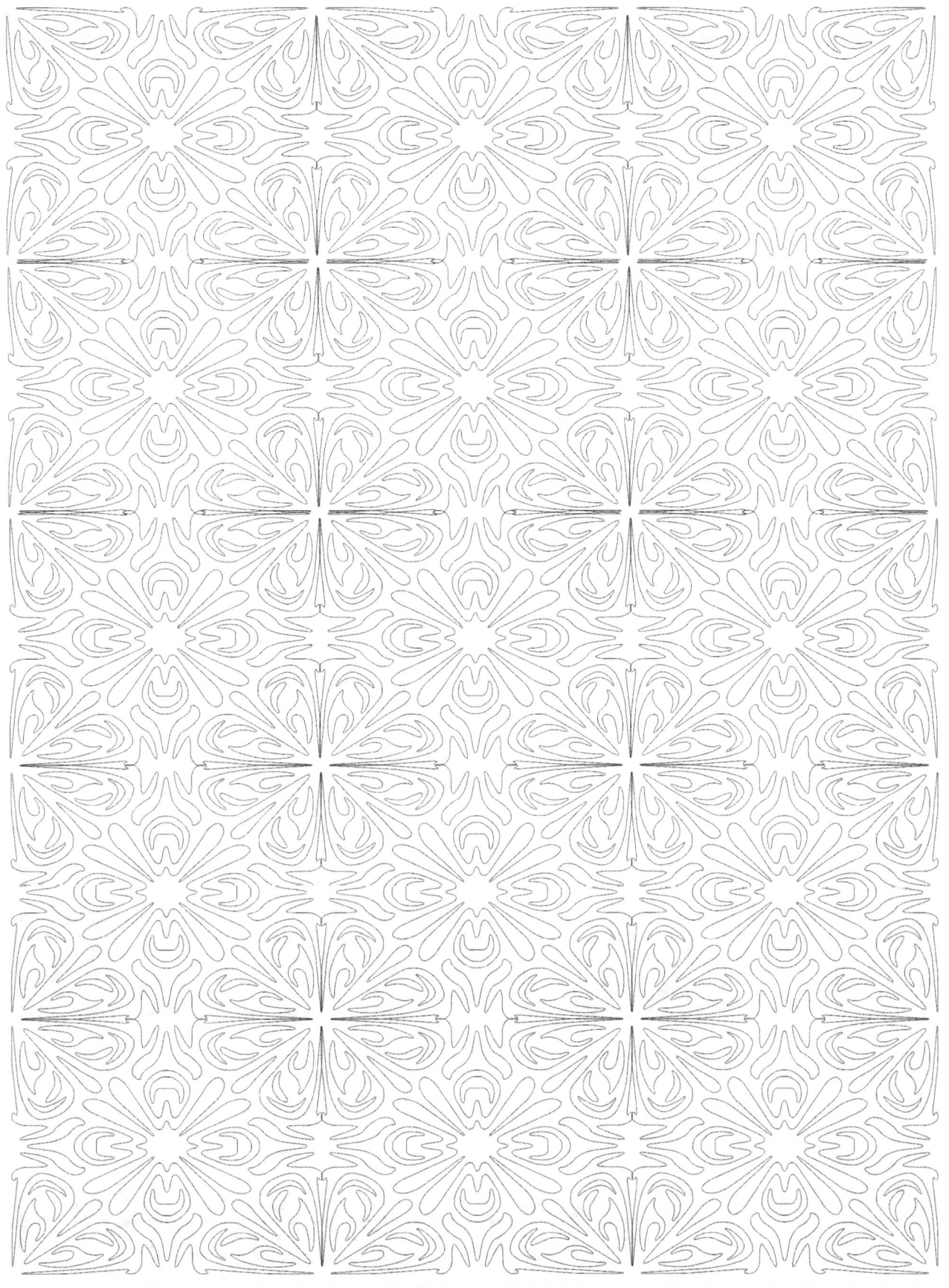

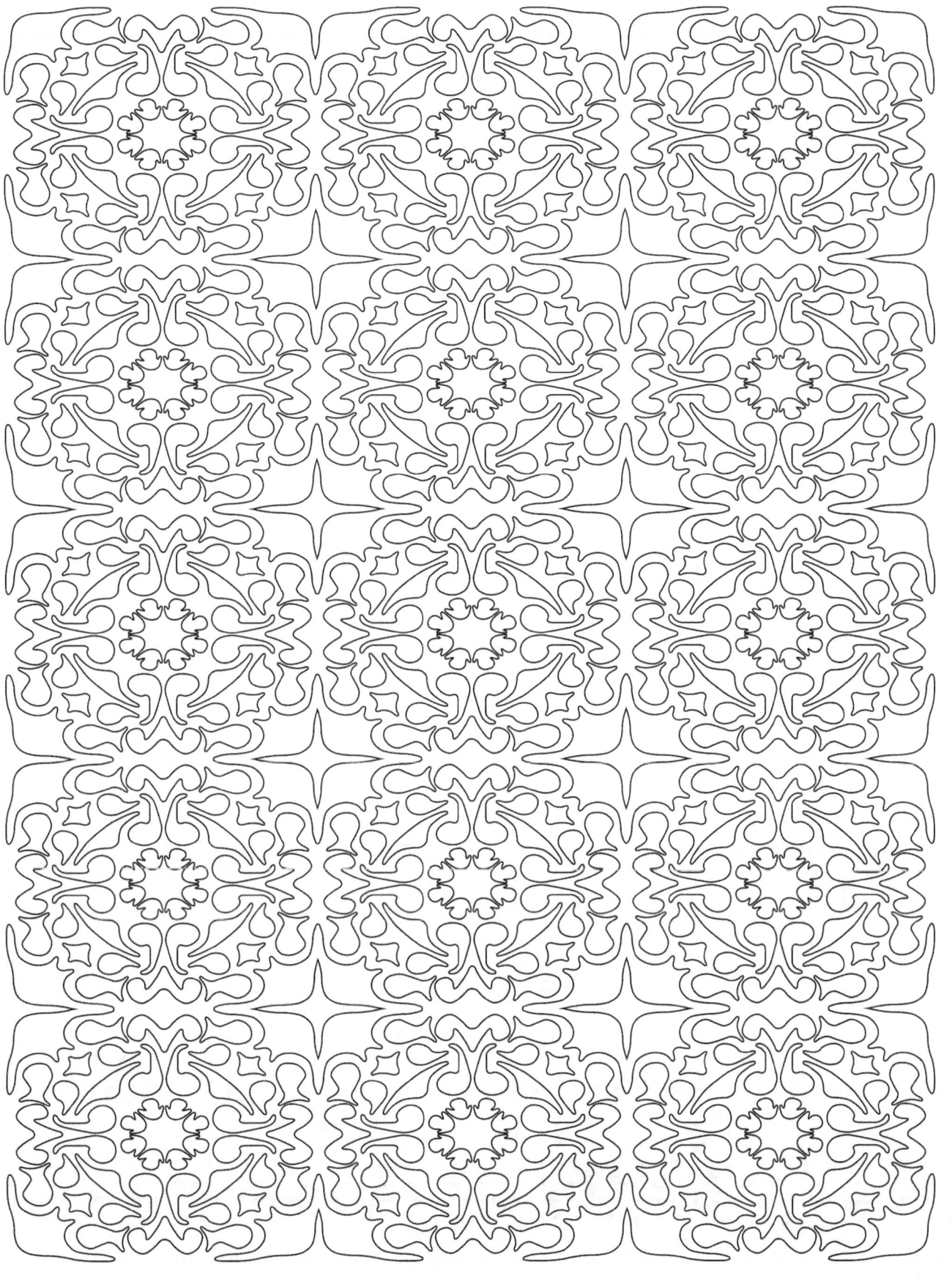

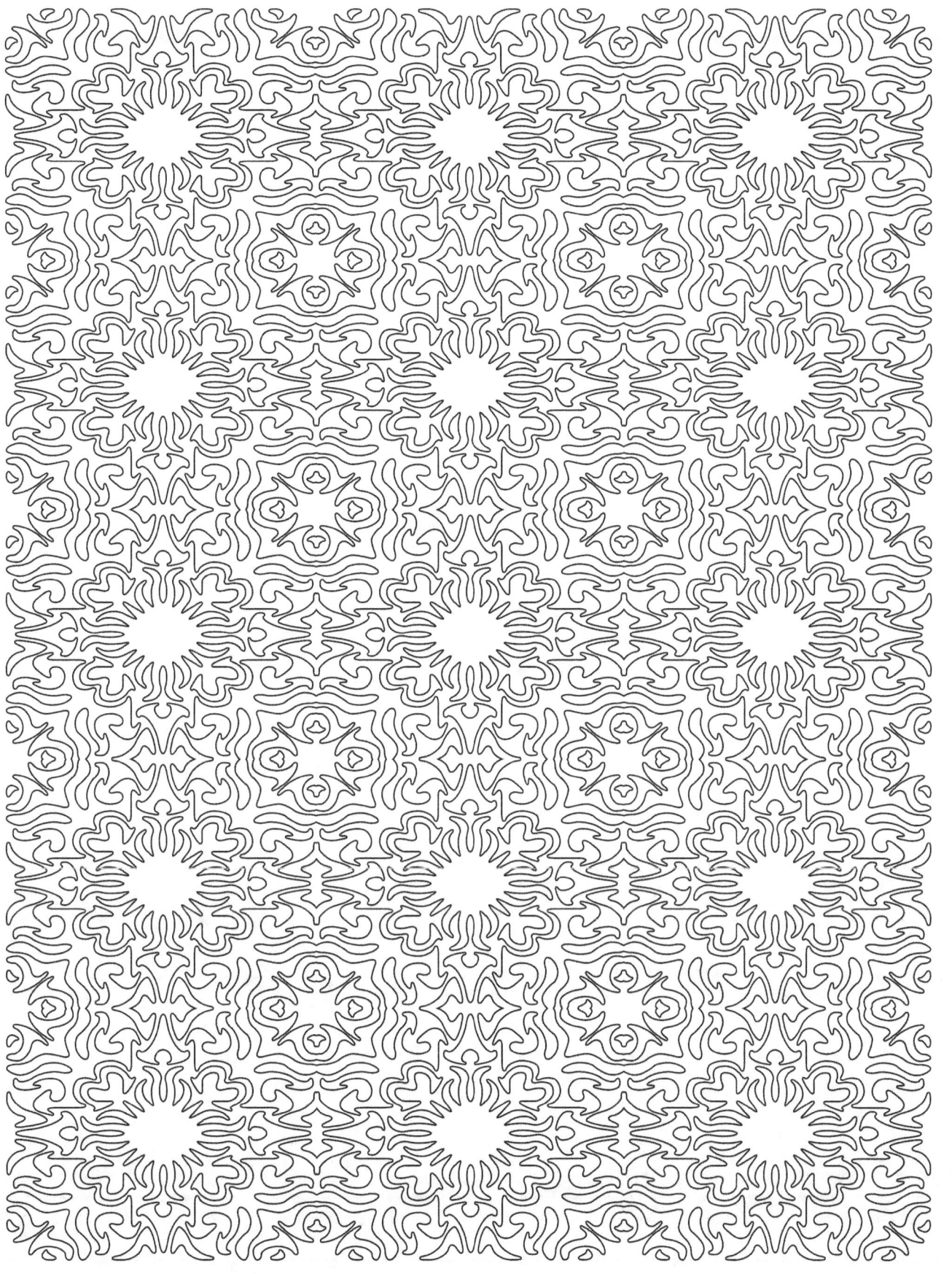

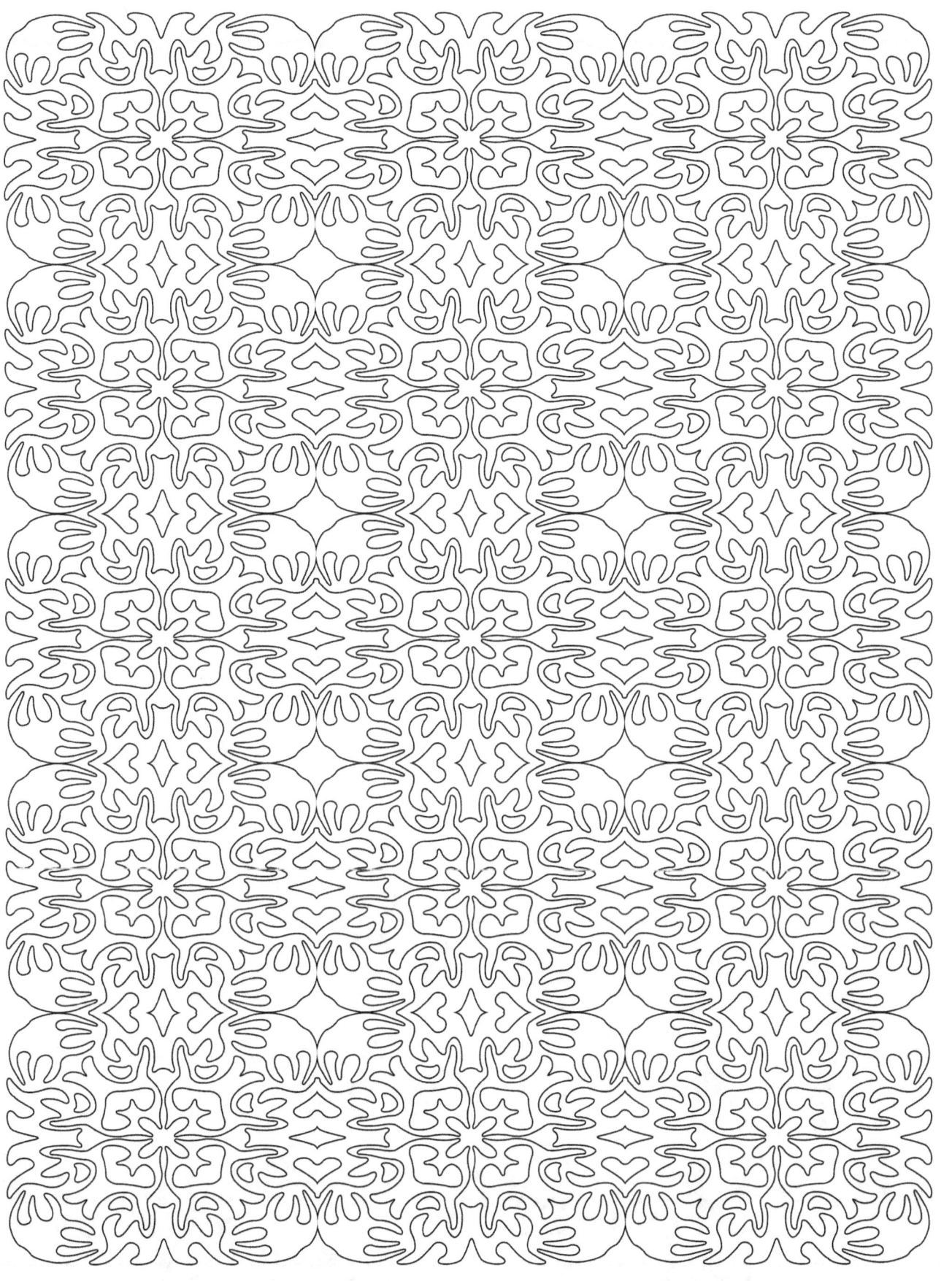

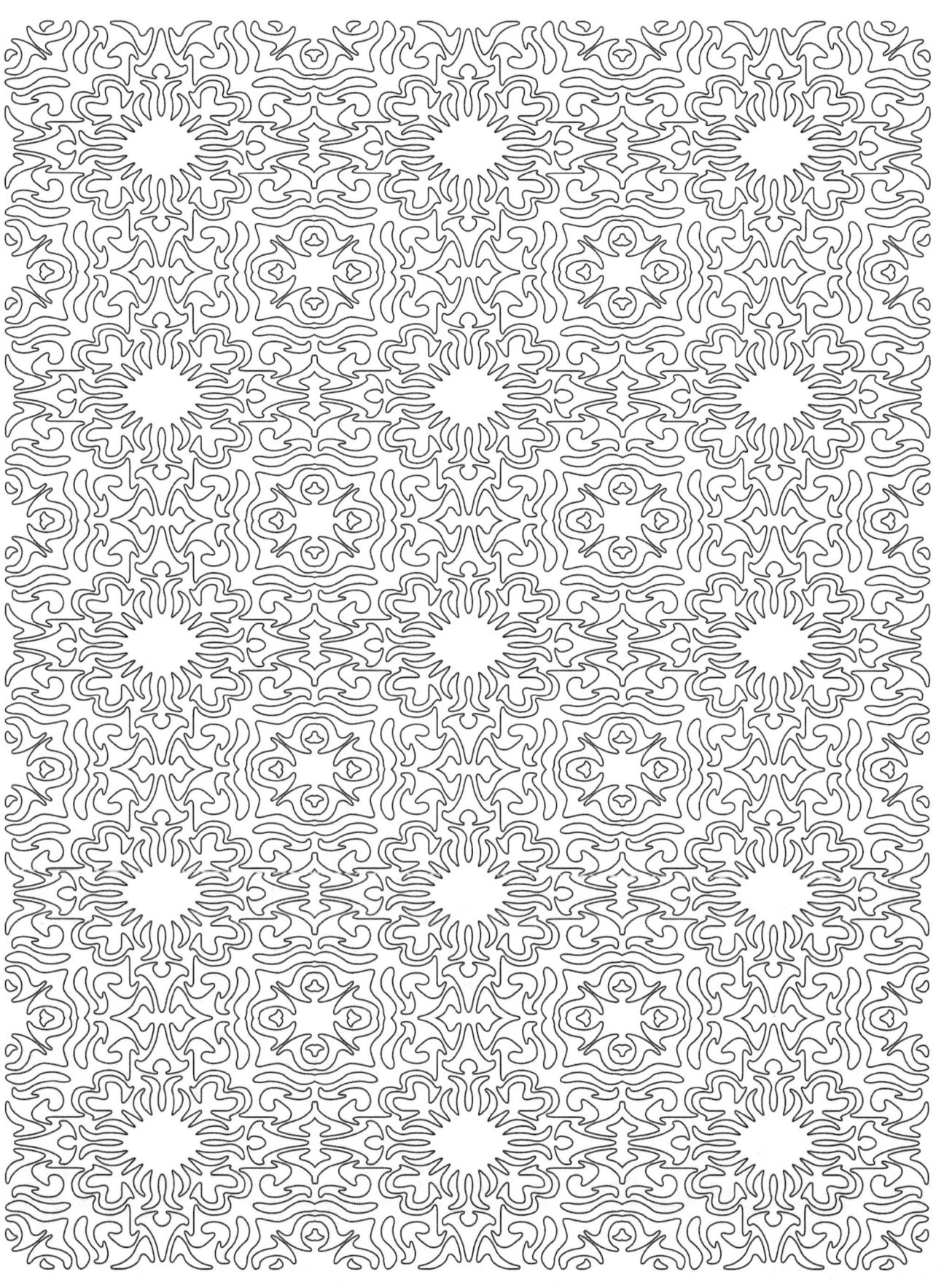

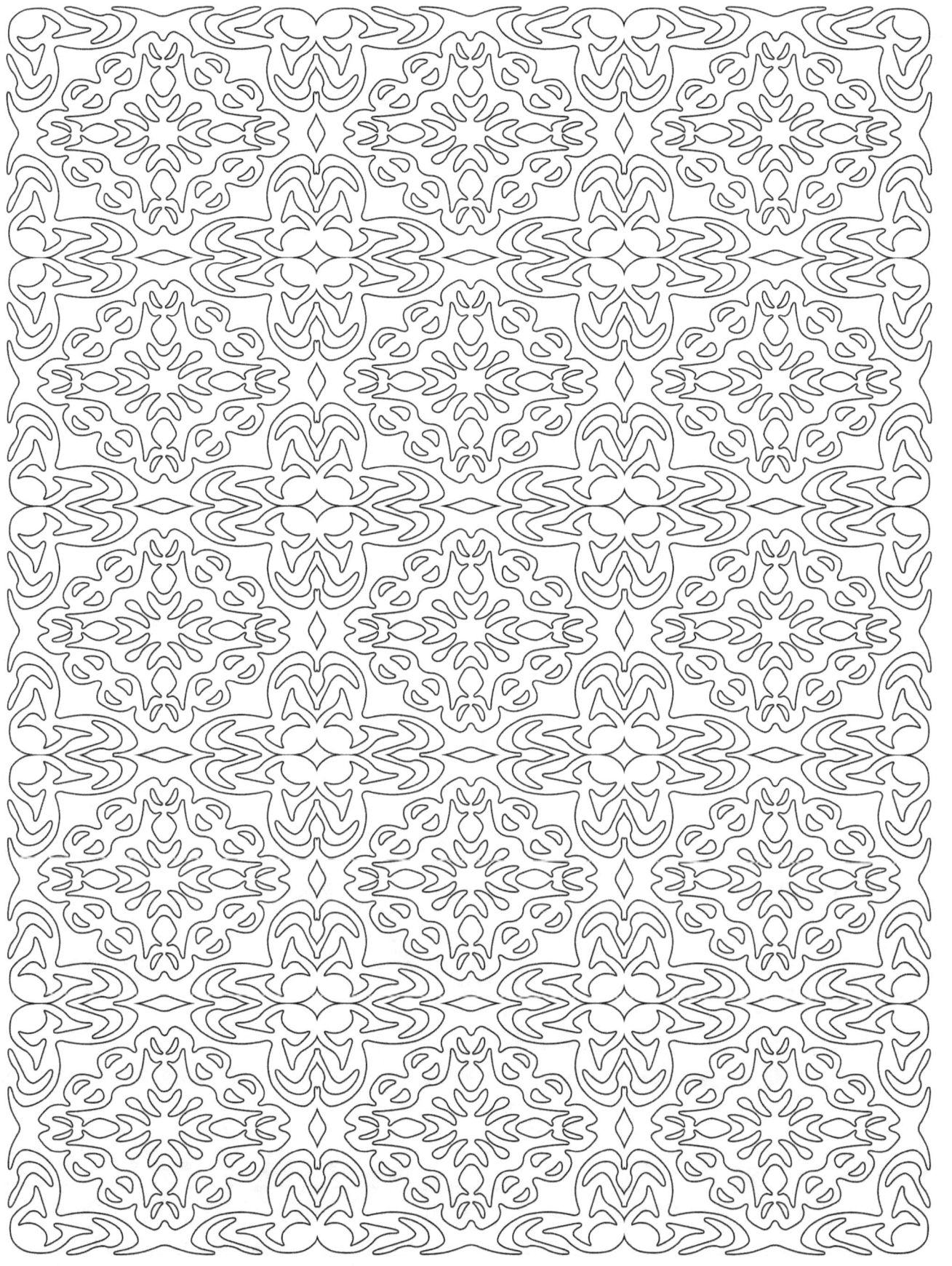

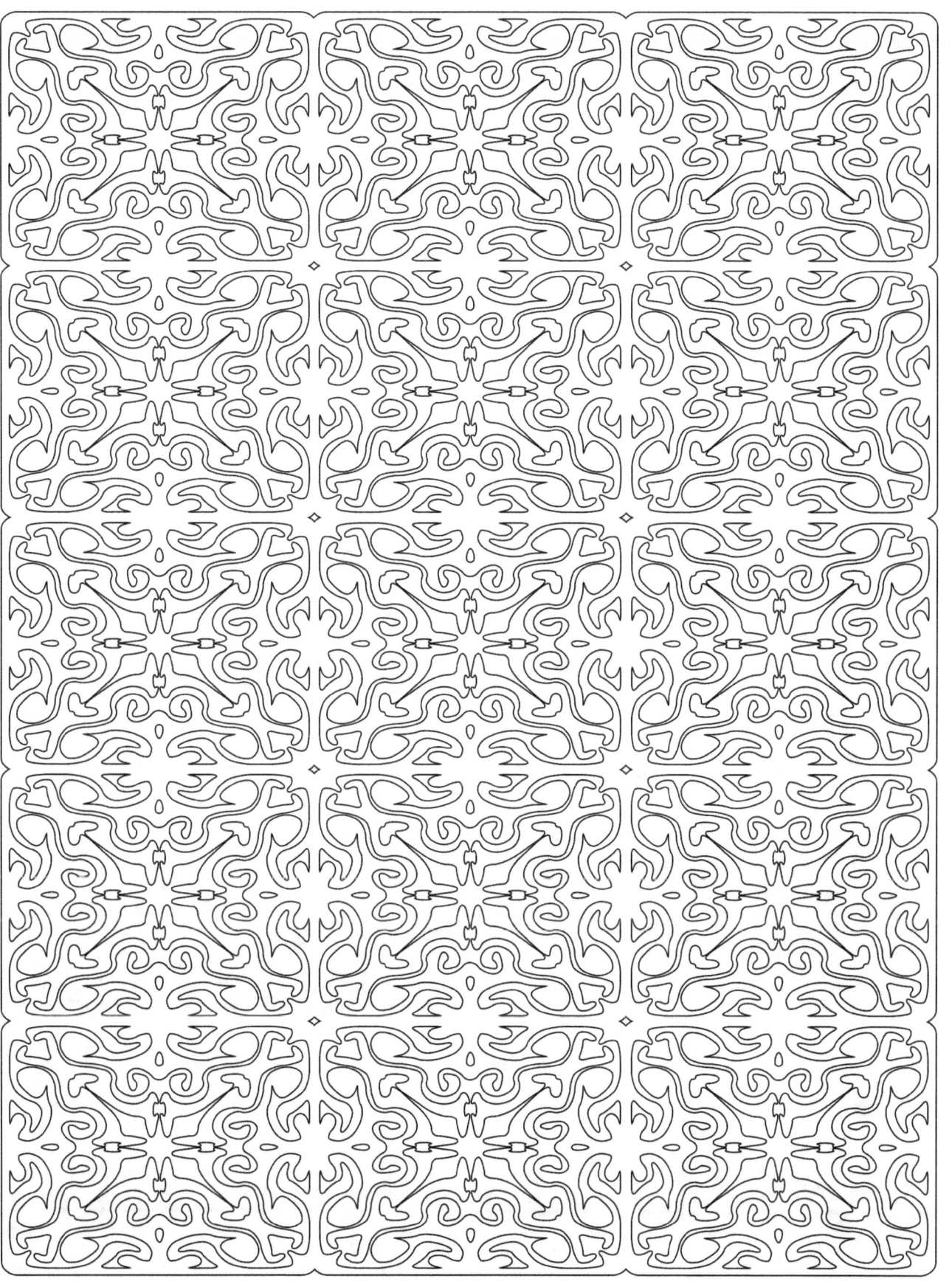

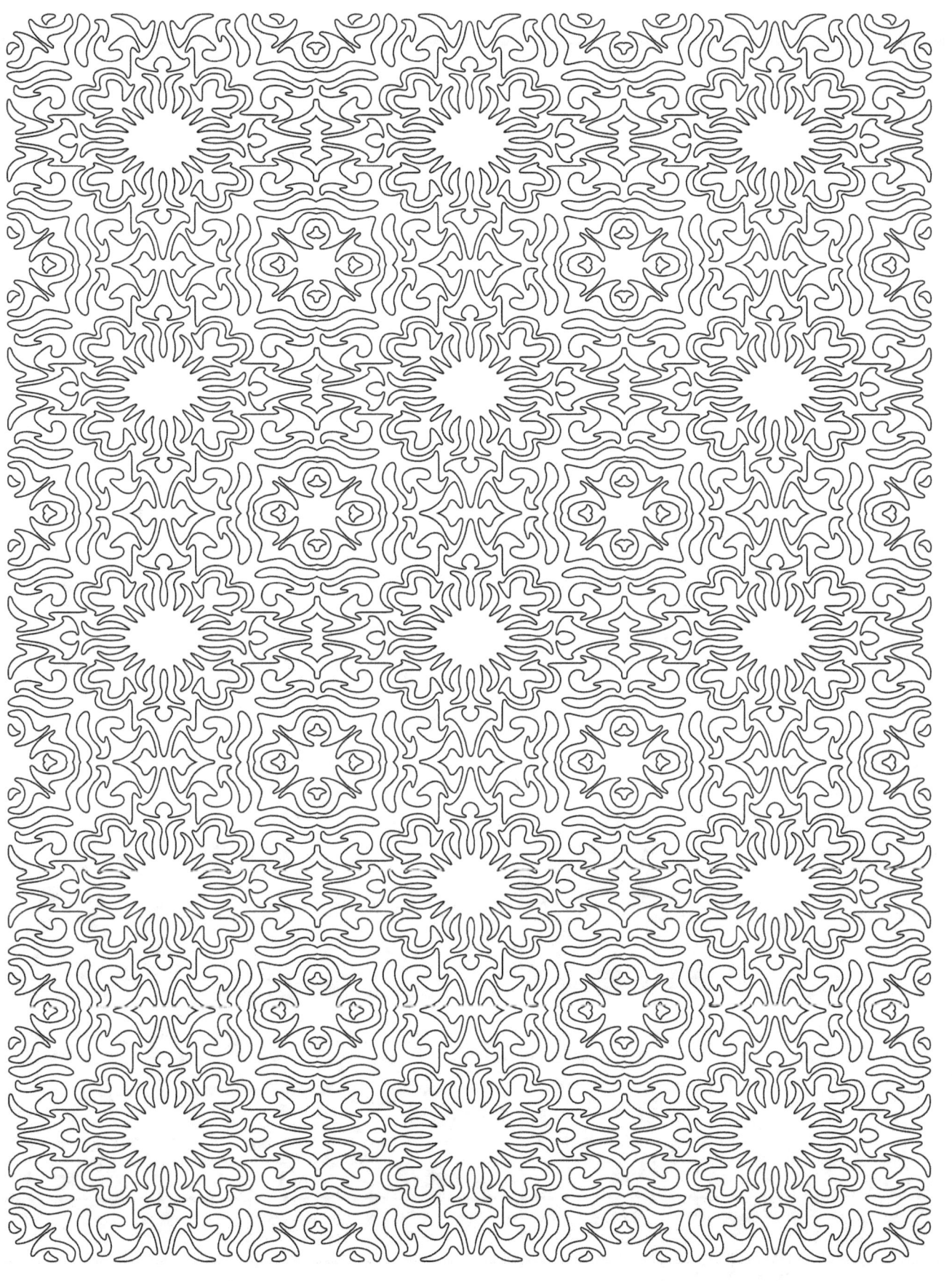

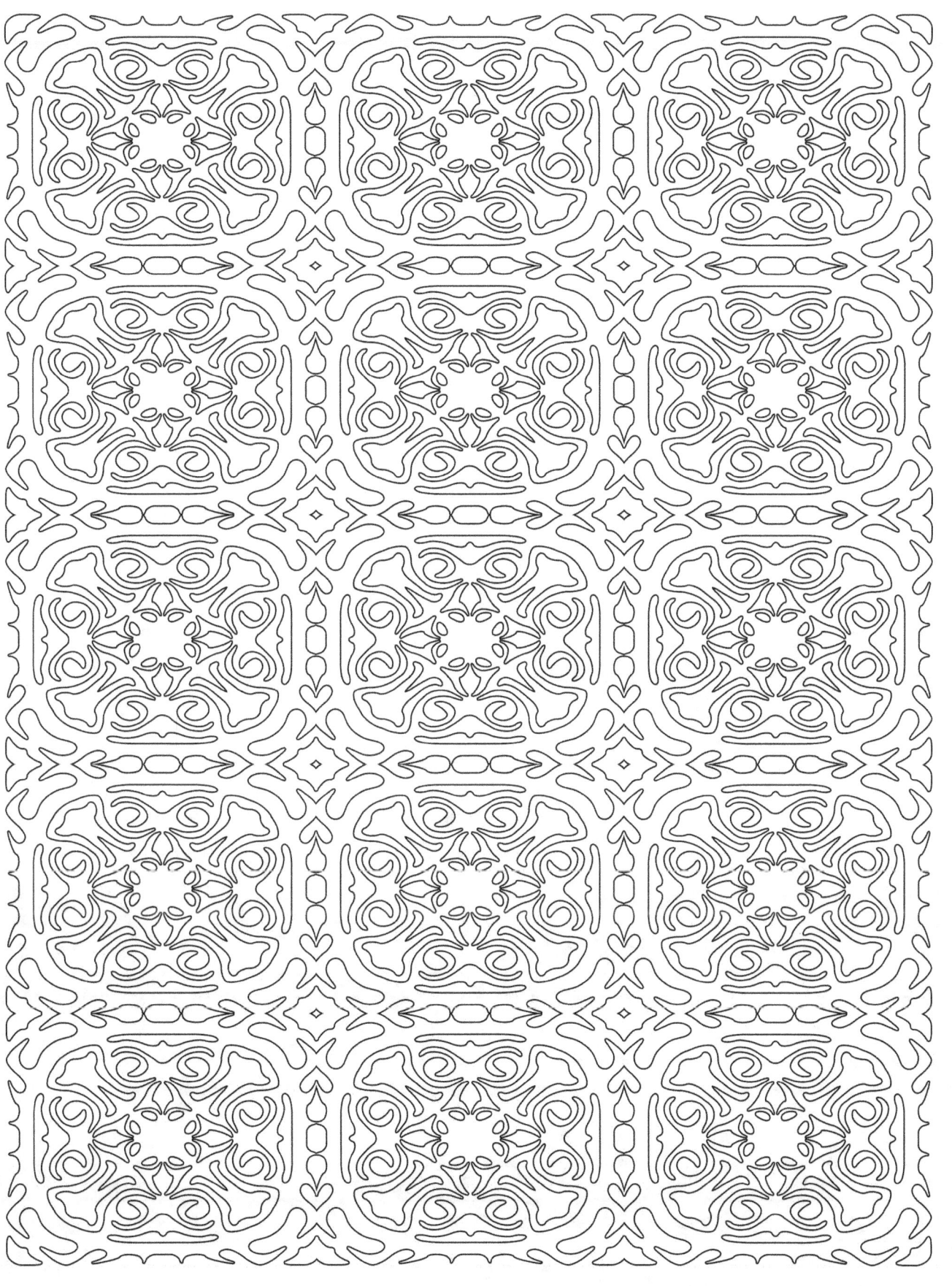

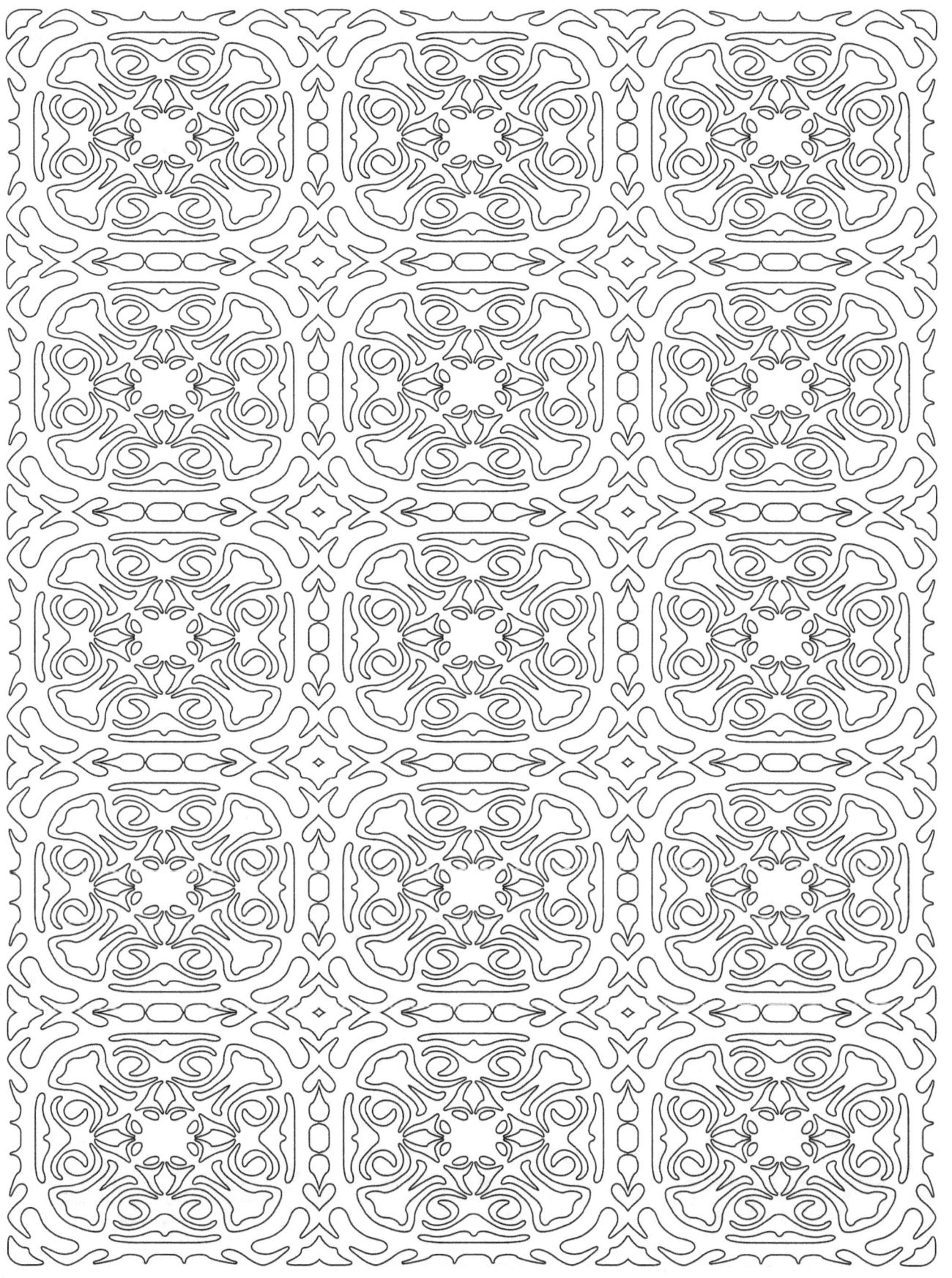

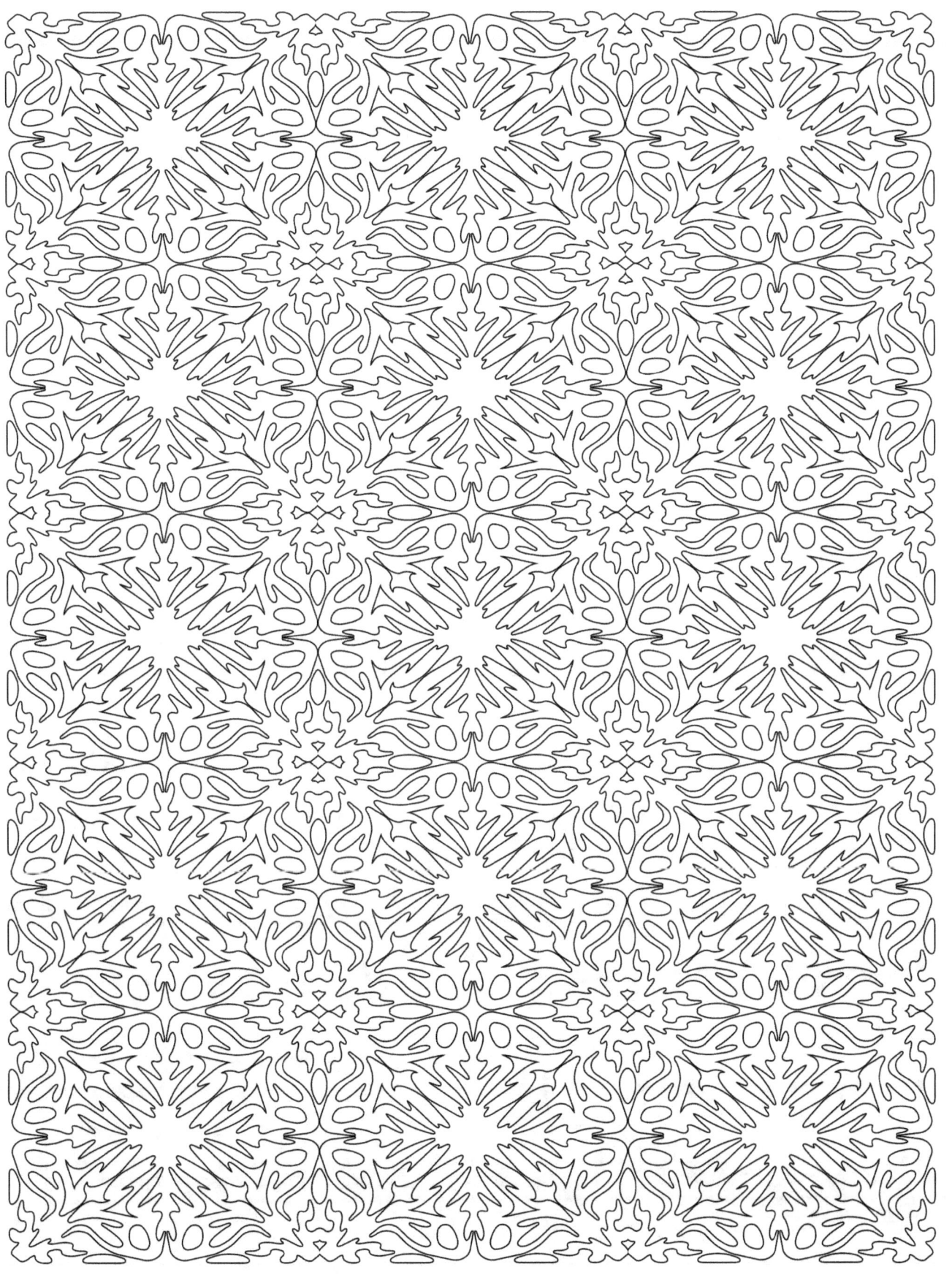

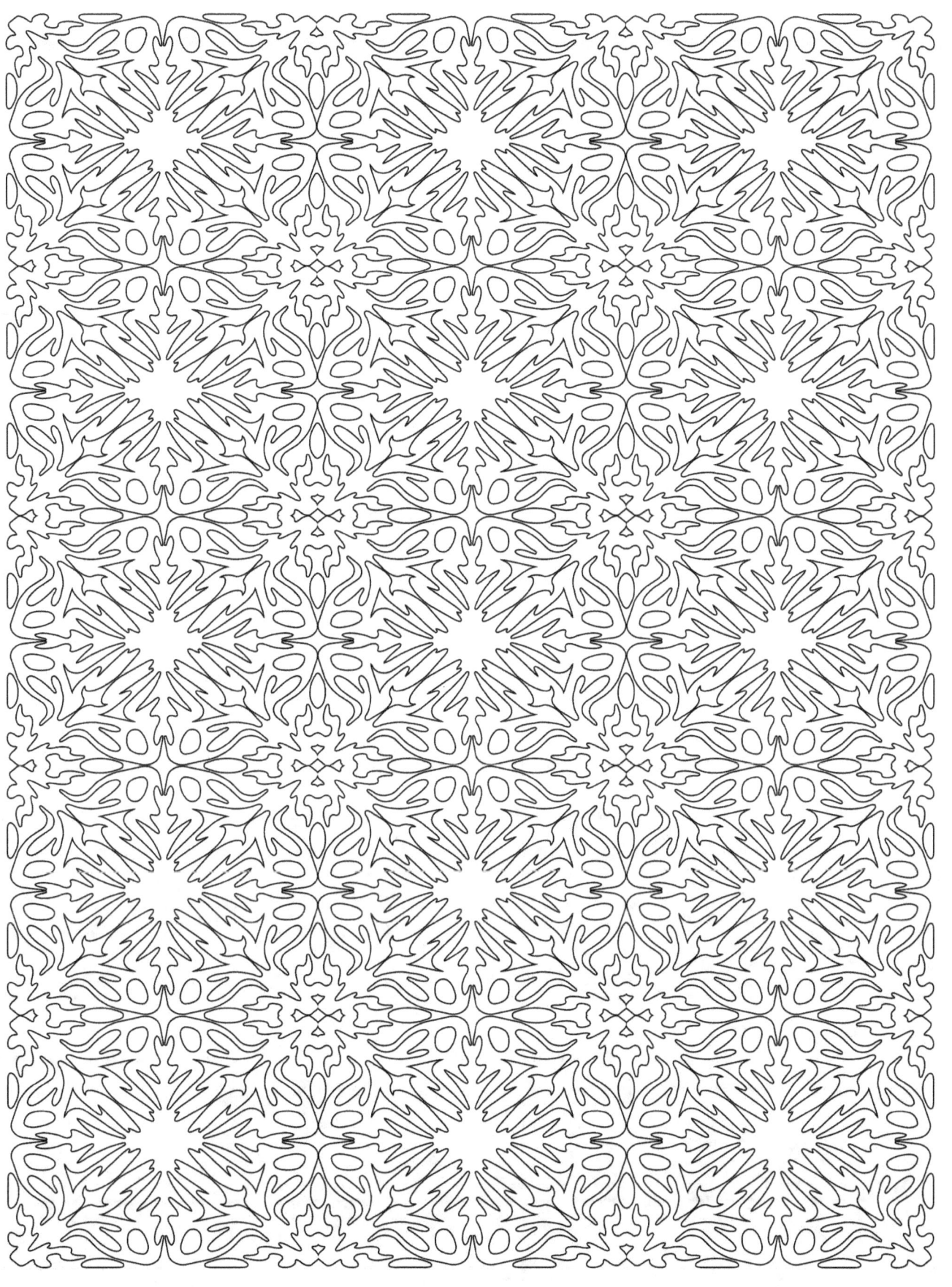

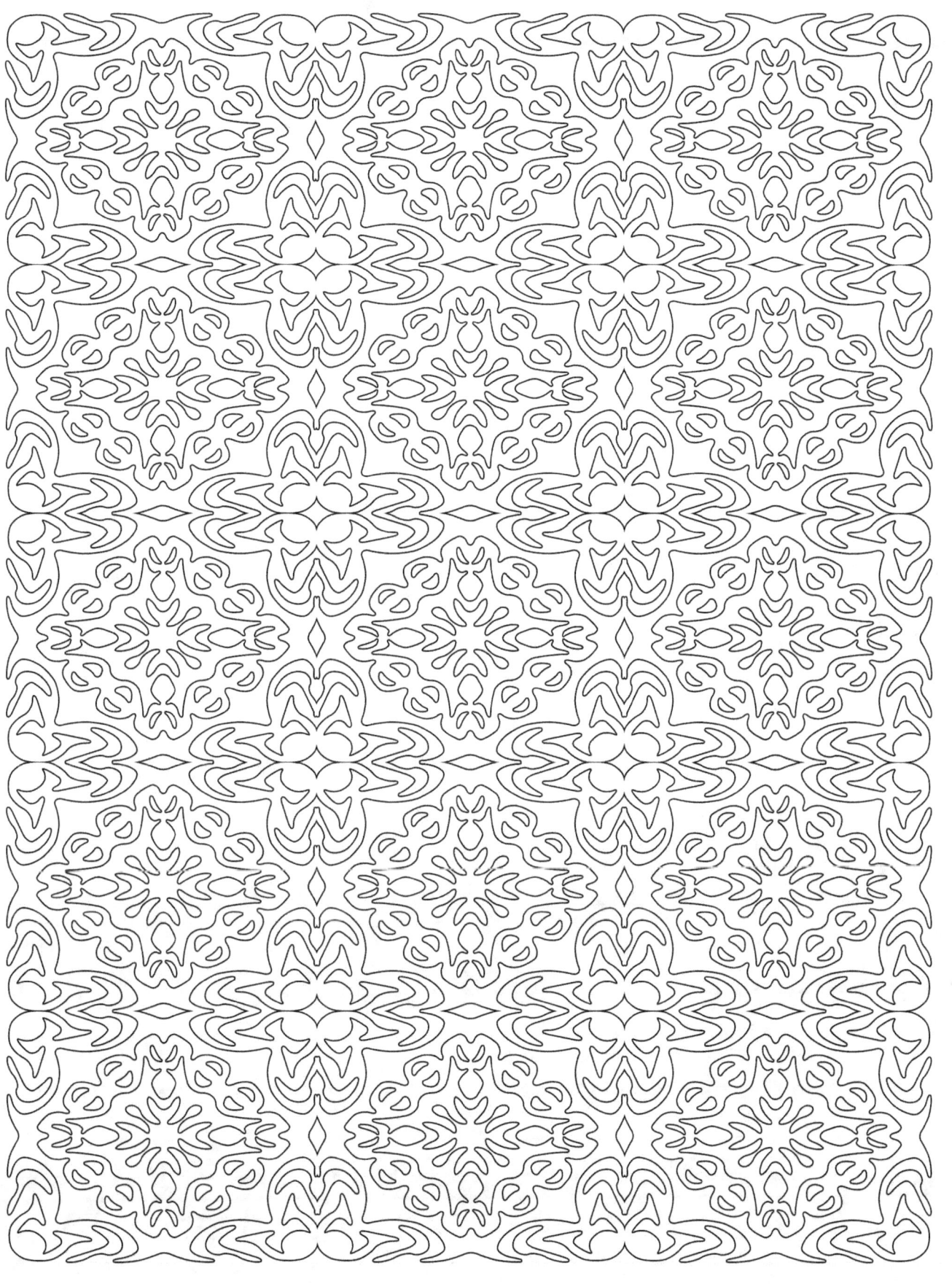

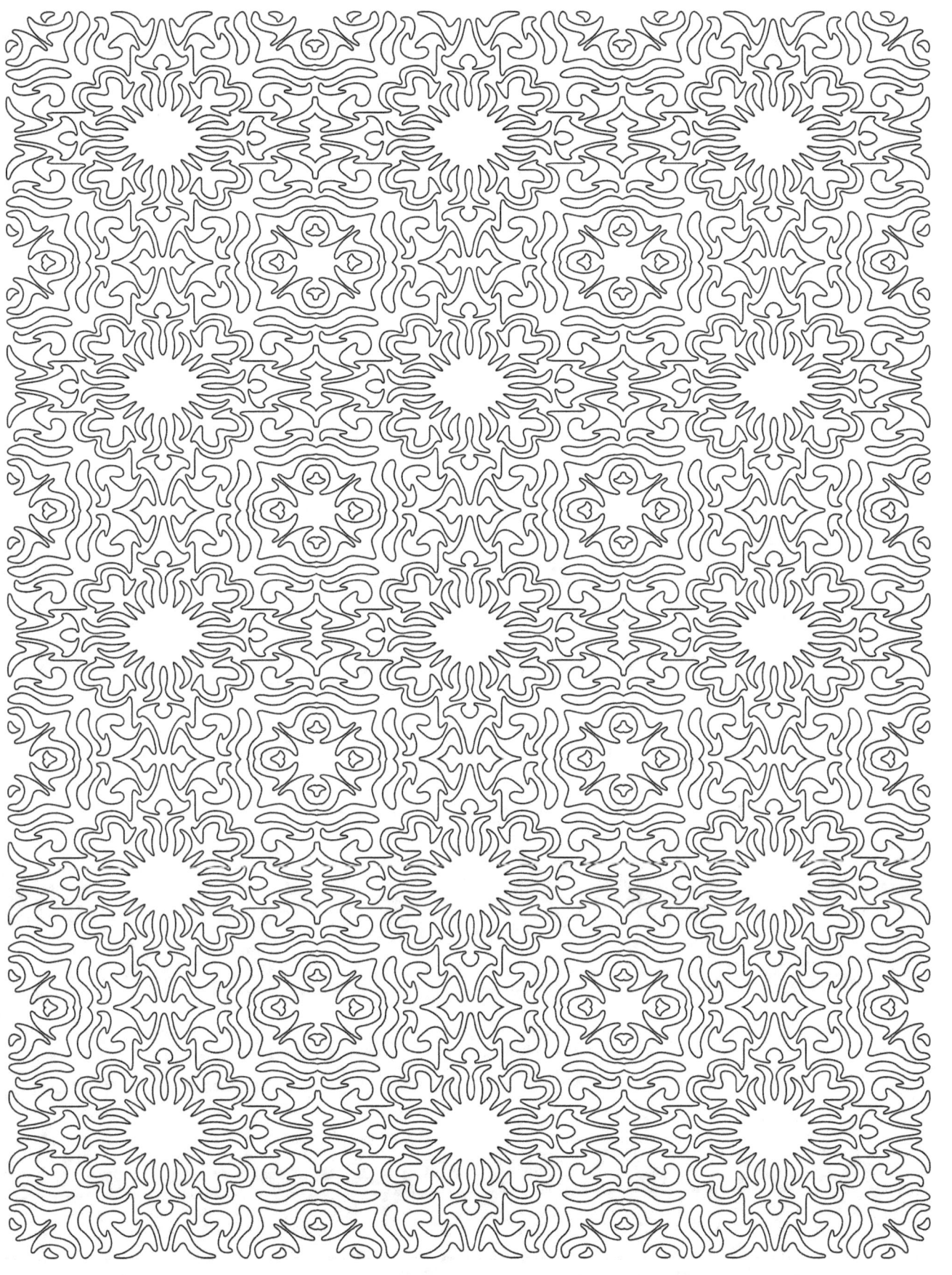

# Final Words

Best wishes in your endeavors!

www.ingramcontent.com/pod-product-compliance
Lightning Source LLC
Chambersburg PA
CBHW082355220526
45470CB00008B/2756